# Managing Information Security Breaches

Studies from real life

**Second edition**

# Managing Information Security Breaches

## Studies from real life

Second edition

MICHAEL KRAUSZ

Every possible effort has been made to ensure that the information contained in this book is accurate at the time of going to press, and the publisher and the author cannot accept responsibility for any errors or omissions, however caused. Any opinions expressed in this book are those of the author, not the publisher. Websites identified are for reference only, not endorsement, and any website visits are at the reader's own risk. No responsibility for loss or damage occasioned to any person acting, or refraining from action, as a result of the material in this publication can be accepted by the publisher or the author.

Apart from any fair dealing for the purposes of research or private study, or criticism or review, as permitted under the Copyright, Designs and Patents Act 1988, this publication may only be reproduced, stored or transmitted, in any form, or by any means, with the prior permission in writing of the publisher or, in the case of reprographic reproduction, in accordance with the terms of licences issued by the Copyright Licensing Agency. Enquiries concerning reproduction outside those terms should be sent to the publisher at the following address:

IT Governance Publishing
IT Governance Limited
Unit 3, Clive Court
Bartholomew's Walk
Cambridgeshire Business Park
Ely, Cambridgeshire
CB7 4EA
United Kingdom

www.itgovernance.co.uk

© Michael Krausz 2010, 2015
The author has asserted the rights of the author under the Copyright, Designs and Patents Act, 1988, to be identified as the author of this work.

First published in the United Kingdom in 2010
by IT Governance Publishing: ISBN 978-1-84928-094-5

Second edition published in 2015
ISBN: 978-1-84928-595-7

# FOREWORD

In 1992, a business acquaintance of mine introduced me to something he called 'the ultimate book on information security'. It turned out to be a guide written by a retired NSA officer with a tendency to talk a little bit more than would probably have been allowed in the terms of the NDAs he had once signed. This, of course, was all the more appreciated by those listening to him. The book focused entirely on written information, and had originally been published in the late 80s or early 90s, a time when I started to use punch card paper as notepaper because there was no longer any use for it in the large IT centres. Much as I respected the retired NSA officer, I felt uncomfortable because the book, even though it was only about 20 years old then, was hopelessly outdated and old fashioned. The way of working with information had changed so much since the time it was written that, early on in my career, I felt that I had to look elsewhere for guidance than to retired NSA officers.

Nowadays, with the ISO27000 family, general information and guidance on how to establish and preserve information security (IS) are readily available for purchase. This is not quite the case when it comes to the question of what to do 'if something happens'. Feeling that the market is not properly served, I thought that it would be valuable to provide the readership with insights on how cyber-investigations are conducted, and on what to do in the event of an incident. This book aims to go right to the heart of what needs to be discussed, carried out and learned from an

*Foreword*

information security incident, covering the full breadth of issues that arise when the worst comes to the worst.

This guide is aimed at CSOs, CISOs, IT security managers, CIOs and, last but not least, CEOs. It particularly addresses personnel in non-IT roles, in an effort to make this unwieldy subject more comprehensible to those who, in a worst-case scenario, will be on the receiving end of requests for six- or seven-figure excess budgets to cope with severe incidents.

This edition has been updated to reflect the transition from ISO27001:2005 to ISO27001:2013. All content related to or referring to "ISO27001" is in accordance with the current version, ISO27001:2013.

# PREFACE

The aim of this book is twofold. Firstly, it provides a general discussion of what information security breaches are, how they can be treated, and what ISO27001 offers in that respect, illustrated with details of real-life information security incidents and breaches.

Secondly, it will form a 'first line of defence' for the reader who is affected by an incident and is looking for guidance and direction.

The Pocket Guide companion to this book summarises all the major points and aims to be a concise reference work for the avoidance and treatment of information security breaches. This book, however, deals with the aspects of information security breaches in extensive detail, with an emphasis on the word 'extensive'. The author wanted to make sure that nothing was overlooked, and everything is explained down to the last nut and bolt – or, at least, the last nuts and bolts that can still make a difference to the final outcome of a breach.

You do not have to read the book strictly from beginning to end. You could start with the case studies in Part 2 for some real-life scare stories, then proceed to Part 1 for a structured overview of risk management, followed by Part 3 to study a sample treatment process. The sequence followed by the three parts of the book, however, leads the reader from learning what is relevant about risk in general, to real-life stories about risks that have materialised, then going on to learn what can be done to effectively and efficiently handle breaches once they have materialised.

# ABOUT THE AUTHOR

Michael Krausz studied Physics, Computer Science and Law at the Vienna University of Technology, Vienna University and Webster University. Combining his two main hobbies, investigations and computers, he has, over the last 20 years, become an accomplished professional investigator, IT expert and ISO27001 auditor. He has investigated over a hundred cases of information security breaches, usually connected with varying degrees of white-collar crime.

He has delivered over 5,000 hours of professional and academic training, and has provided consulting or investigation services in 21 countries so far.

# ACKNOWLEDGEMENTS

I gratefully acknowledge the assistance of IT Governance Ltd, without whom this book would not have seen the light of the bookshelf, real or virtual. I would also like to acknowledge the direct or indirect support of friends, colleagues and business partners. Special thanks go out to Chris Evans and Michael Wang who both provided much cherished feedback on the first version of the original manuscript. Further thanks should be extended to Angela Wilde for managing the first edition of this book and to Vicki Utting for managing its second edition.

Alan Calder and Steve Watkins of IT Governance were essential in bringing it to life in the first place by acknowledging that this somewhat uncomfortable subject needs to be tackled.

# CONTENTS

Introduction ........................................................................ 1

Part 1 – General ................................................................. 3

Chapter 1: Why Risk does Not Depend on Company Size ........................................................................................ 3
    Risk effect ...................................................................... 8
    Propagation of damage (downstream effects) ............... 8
    Culture ............................................................................ 9
    Information security staff ............................................ 10
    Cash reserves / cash at hand ........................................ 10
    Ability to improvise / make quick decisions .............. 11
    Preparedness ................................................................ 11
    Contacts with authority ............................................... 12

Chapter 2: Getting your Risk Profile Right ................... 15
    Intuitive risk analysis .................................................. 16
    Formal risk analysis .................................................... 18
    Residual risks .............................................................. 40

Chapter 3: What is a Breach? ......................................... 43
    Confidentiality breach ................................................ 45
    Availability breach ...................................................... 46
    Integrity breach ........................................................... 47

Chapter 4: General Avoidance and Mitigation Strategies ........................................................................... 55
    Introduction – general aspects, avoidance and related ISO27001 controls ..................................................... 55
    People .......................................................................... 56
    Processes ..................................................................... 71
    Technology ................................................................. 80
    Strategies and tactics for treating breaches ................ 89

## Contents

Dimensions of treatment / mitigation of information
security breaches ............................................................... 96

**Part 2 – Case studies** .......................................................... **101**

**Chapter 5: Notes from the Field** .................................... **101**
    Privacy ................................................................................ 101
    Cost .................................................................................... 102
    The practicalities of surveillance ...................................... 102
    The truth vs. company policy ............................................ 104
**Chapter 6: Motives and Reasons** .................................. **105**
    Greed .................................................................................. 105
    Despair ............................................................................... 106
    Revenge .............................................................................. 106
    Business advantage ............................................................ 108
**Chapter 7: Case Studies from Small Companies** ........ **111**
    Foreword to the case studies ............................................ 111
    The stolen backup ............................................................. 111
    Eavesdropping on faxes .................................................... 115
    A stolen laptop .................................................................. 117
**Chapter 8: Case Studies from Medium-sized Companies**
............................................................................................. **123**
    A case of intrigue – the missing contract ........................ 123
    The sales manager who changed jobs ............................. 127
    The project manager who became a friend, and then an
    enemy ................................................................................ 131
    The lost customers – how a sales manager cost a company
    10% of revenue ................................................................. 136
    The flood – how not to learn about risk management ... 142
**Chapter 9: Case Studies from Large Corporations** .... **147**
    Who wants my data? – a case of data theft .................... 147
    Who wants my data? – a more complicated case .......... 154
    Hard disk for sale – beware of your contractors ............ 163

# Contents

Unauthorised domain links – it is easy to harm a company's reputation ..................................................... 166
The trusted guard who was not ........................................ 169
Insider badmouthing ........................................................ 172
The software vulnerability that was not – a case of blackmail ......................................................................... 174

**Part 3 – A Sample Treatment Process** ....................... 181

**Chapter 10: A Sample Treatment Process** ................ 181
   Step 1   Gather information ............................................. 181
   Step 2   Determine extent and damage ........................ 183
   Step 3   Establish and conduct investigation .............. 184
   Step 4   Determine mitigation ....................................... 185
   Step 5   Implement mitigation ...................................... 187
   Step 6   Follow up on investigation results ................. 187
   Step 7   Determine degree of resolution achieved ...... 188

**Abbreviations and Acronyms** ..................................... 189

**ITG Resources** ............................................................. 191

# INTRODUCTION

Breaches of information security are not a new phenomenon, but the means of perpetrating such breaches have changed considerably over the years. Leaking information has always been an issue, but the speed and effectiveness with which breaches of information security can occur, and the potential magnitude of harm caused in today's computer age, are disturbing and, moreover, typically favour the perpetrator, not the victim.

Bearing in mind the dependency of modern companies on their IT systems, it is clear that special care needs to be taken to keep systems safe and secure. This book focuses solely on the aspects of re-establishing safety and security once, despite all measures taken, a breach has occurred. It puts breaches of information security in the context of ISO27001 which, since its inception in the late 80s as British Standard 7799, has demonstrated that it can provide a framework of requirements well suited to the effective implementation of countermeasures and measures designed to protect information in all its forms, whether on paper, in speech or in the IT field.

This book describes a process and its elements for the treatment of severe breaches, and places them in the context the relevant ISO27001 controls. It provides input for decision making and for breach classification, and offers case studies to enable the reader to explore how other companies were affected and what they did (or did not do) upon falling victim to a breach.

These case studies have been carefully selected from the case collection of the author, and some cases have been

## Introduction

included that entered the public domain, but where the author has background knowledge. Naturally, some facts regarding the identities of companies and locations had to be changed to protect the companies and their business. All the basic facts relevant to the breach and to each case are true, and happened as described.

This book is structured along a precise line of thought: definitions and general subjects in Part 1, real-life case studies in Part 2, and what to do to resolve a breach in Part 3.

Part 1 serves as an introduction by defining the terms 'risk' and 'breach' and putting them into the context of a risk management framework, as well as describing general avoidance strategies as contained in ISO27001. This part can be seen either as a means for the reader to complement existing knowledge, or as a starting point for those who have not yet delved deeply into matters of risk management.

Part 2 comprises a number of case studies to provide the reader with real-life stories of breaches and subsequent events. ISO27001 even states that a company should try to learn from its own incidents and those of others. This, in the real world, turns out to be rather difficult as companies have a natural tendency not to be too open about such incidents. The author feels that we are closing a gap with these case studies, all of which have been taken from a collection of more than 100 cases in which he was personally involved. Part 2 describes the events, and includes a full explanation of what actions were taken, why, and what the outcome was, including lessons learned.

Part 3 provides a sample treatment process in descriptive form.

# PART 1 – GENERAL

## CHAPTER 1: WHY RISK DOES NOT DEPEND ON COMPANY SIZE

What is the real worth of the USB stick you just bought for £15? After a year, if you included it as a short-term cost item in your accounts, it would not be worth anything. On the other hand, if it contained all the latest data of your research project which was bound to pay off in a couple of years, then it would be worth pretty close to infinity or, at least, the future of your company.

It is not easy to define risk or what taking a risk really means. Sometimes people try to use probabilities and ALEs (Annual Loss Expectancy); sometimes damage or the propagation of damage along a business process is included; sometimes risk is described as a vector of vulnerabilities and threats (which is the favoured way to see it in the information security world); and sometimes it is described by the options available for action. We will not try to give you a comprehensive, all-encompassing definition. We just want to make a couple of points: that risk permeates your company or corporation from top to bottom, from head to toe and, particularly, that risk and information security risks do not in any way depend on the size of your company.

This latter point is important, as companies sometimes tend to underestimate their exposure and to overestimate their resiliency (cf. 'too big to fail' as a banking sector

## 1: Why Risk does Not Depend on Company Size

paradigm). There is no such thing as 'too big to fail' in the information security world; a well-organised incident can bring down empires or, at least, damage them so much that recovery can take years, if it even remains affordable. It is true, however, that there are distinct differences in how companies can cope with, and avoid, incidents. Some avoidance and treatment options are largely based on size, but, then again, size is measured here as in 'cash available', 'reserves available', 'speed to implement treatment options', and so on. Company size, measured, for instance, by number of employees or locations, does not really mean anything in regard to information security risks.

Let us briefly state the definition of company sizes as used in this book. For our purposes, a company with up to 100 employees is considered small; 100 to 1,000 is considered medium; and 1,000+ is considered large. For the sake of clarity, we will not take into account revenues, cash or profits, and we will not consider that these sizes may all be considered small in some countries or may fit another country's business structure perfectly. As a real-life example, consider an actual company in the medical sector, with only 300 employees, that makes more than a billion euros a year selling its specialised devices.

Let us, first of all, give a brief definition of risk in the information security world. The most commonly used, most practical, approach today is to define risk as a vector of vulnerabilities and threats, with some likelihood and damage levels associated later. A vulnerability is a weakness that can be exploited by an associated threat and is based on properties of the system(s) and process(es) you are using. Vulnerabilities are inherent in IT systems, your physical location, and your processes, because of their design and their inherent characteristics.

# 1: Why Risk does Not Depend on Company Size

A threat is an event or process that can (ab)use these vulnerabilities to cause harm to the confidentiality, availability or integrity of your system (all assets considered as one) or systems. A threat can be man-made or natural; its associated damage can be caused by malicious intent, by accident or by technical failure.

If a vulnerability has a corresponding threat, then a risk clearly exists. The level of risk will depend on the measures already in place, and will be higher, the less effective these measures are. If a vulnerability does not have a corresponding threat, or if a threat exists, but without corresponding vulnerability, then the risk resulting from such combinations is simply zero. Once it has been determined whether a risk exists or not, one will usually factor in the following:

- the likelihood of the risk materialising;
- the direct damage caused by the risk materialising;
- indirect damage throughout a chain of business processes;
- the cost of mitigating measures;
- business priorities of mitigating measures.

In bringing together all of the above, a risk analysis is duly completed (more on that in the following chapter) which will show management what the situation of the company is, and what can be done about it in both the short and the long term. But, to return to the subject of this chapter, none of these factors depend in any way on company size. There is only one question of paramount importance that illustrates our point:

*How much damage will this particular risk do to my company?*

## 1: Why Risk does Not Depend on Company Size

If you look at some risks, for example, the German Baseline Protection Manual's list of threats and vulnerabilities, you will find that some risks can hit you severely, while others are irrelevant, but none of these will have anything to do with the size of your company.

Some risks are almost trivial, such as a CEO's child running some CD in the office and unwittingly importing a virus; some risks are elaborate and require malicious intent, such as social engineering or corporate espionage; but, as this example shows, it could happen anywhere, and it could do the same fundamental damage to any type of company (though larger companies tend to be better prepared).

Consider research-driven companies for a moment. There are large pharmaceutical companies and technology businesses that invest billions in research, and competitors who think that stealing, rather than investing, would be a good strategy. Hence, a threat for the former companies exists. But there are also a number of medium-sized companies who are leaders within their niche, invest heavily in research on a slightly different scale of millions instead of billions, and therefore have the same fundamental risk profile. Based on their cash reserves, a medium-sized company may even be better equipped to survive a fundamental information security breach; in general, though, the level of preparedness tends to be less evolved, but, nevertheless, the nature of the risk is exactly same and, on a carefully chosen risk level matrix, the risk level would most probably also be the same.

So far, we have focused on the effect of the risk in relation to the company, and demonstrated that the risk does not

# 1: Why Risk does Not Depend on Company Size

depend on the size of the company. Let us look at another aspect: preparedness.

Preparedness for an incident depends not on company size, but, rather, on its culture. That culture can be highly evolved or not present at all, but, again, it will not depend on size. In smaller companies (fewer than 1,000 employees) company culture can be much more refined, and can be carried by a mid-level of highly motivated managers who identify with, or admire, the founder or founding partners. In such companies, personal contact with the owner or founder usually occurs regularly. On the other hand, larger companies (over 1,000 employees) can easily evolve into bureaucracies, where people do only what they are asked to do. In such a culture, establishing a new view on risks, or security as a whole, is difficult and can take some time (often up to two or three years). Furthermore, larger companies have a tendency to underestimate the value of building awareness, and concentrate on measures they perceive as being more cost efficient or just cheaper. For example, one defence sector company thought that, instead of a fully-fledged awareness programme involving classroom training and Q&A sessions, handing out CDs and making staff take an online exam would be enough. Unfortunately, this is not always the best way in which to pass on this kind of information.

Next, we will look at the relevant factors for treating or avoiding information security incidents, and examine whether any of these are connected to company size.

# 1: Why Risk does Not Depend on Company Size

**Risk effect**

As mentioned above, risk effects do not depend on company size for severe risks. Big companies usually do better at keeping a risk from spreading all through the company (downstream effects), but this is countered by the ability of small companies to act promptly and without much bureaucracy. If we measure the risk effect in qualitative terms from 'low' to 'substantial' to 'extreme', then a risk can hit all types of companies equally hard.

Small companies are often less well prepared, and do not quite structure their efforts, adopting a more ad hoc approach, so the effects on them tend to be more disruptive and less controlled than in larger companies which have implemented a fully-fledged information security programme. If we focus on the general effect of any given risk, however, the effects and their range are strikingly similar.

**Propagation of damage (downstream effects)**

Propagation of damage occurs when damage caused by a risk that has materialised propagates through a business process or a number of business processes. Bigger companies tend to have an advantage, as their business processes are generally more tightly controlled, whereas smaller companies usually face severe customer *chagrin* and loss of business if damage propagates through a chain of processes. As an example, consider the following scenario.

A medium-sized bakery produces bread to be used by a fast-food company. Imagine one of the baking machines not working, due to some IT failure. The bread will not be

## 1: Why Risk does Not Depend on Company Size

delivered and, apart from fast-food customers staying hungry (or eating healthily for a change), contractual penalties may be invoked, further elevating the damage level caused by risk materialisation.

In the automotive industry, a failure at one supplier can propagate through the entire chain of production, causing a standstill at the main factory.

### Culture

How risks are seen and treated before they actually materialise is based on a company's culture. In smaller companies, the culture is directly carried by the opinions and attitudes of the IT manager, the managing director, or the owner(s). If the IT manager (there are often no separate IS staff) is on top of their game, this can be advantageous; but if the company still thinks IT is a nuisance as a whole, the result can be totally detrimental.

Having paid the price of establishing their culture through a year-long process, larger companies tend to have the advantage of a more stable culture, which is less dependent on the individuals carrying it; however, even large companies can have an incomplete, or totally absent, view on information security risks, which will then aggravate risk effects.

Again, size does not matter at all, as the culture required to avoid and treat breaches either is, or is not, there. It does not really matter where it came from, but only if it is actually there.

# 1: Why Risk does Not Depend on Company Size

## Information security staff

This is the one case in which big companies clearly win. Smaller companies tend not to have IS teams. If you are lucky, you will find a dedicated IT manager for whom, in very small companies (less than 100 people) this may even be an extra role. You will not usually find dedicated information security staff at small companies. Bigger companies generally set up entire teams of information security experts and, today, in a company with 2,000+ employees you can expect to find 3 to 15 people working exclusively on information security issues. One of these people is likely to have some background in investigation, which will prepare the company better for treating a breach.

## Cash reserves / cash at hand

One of the most important things in treating a breach is to have quite large amounts of cash at one's disposal, in order to be able to start investigations quickly or to buy equipment to resume operations. The amount of money set aside as reserves or in hand, however, does not necessarily depend entirely on company size, as some small companies may have business models that allow them to have large amounts of cash at their disposal, whereas a large company may find itself stripped of cash due to some other business event or a general lack of free cash flow. Larger companies are more likely to have large reserves, but that cannot be taken for granted. In terms of available cash, successful medium-sized companies, which have managed to secure their niche, are generally even richer than bigger companies.

# 1: Why Risk does Not Depend on Company Size

**Ability to improvise / make quick decisions**

This is a winning point for smaller companies as, out of necessity they tend to be better at improvisation after a disaster than large companies, which need any number of signatures to get even simple things done. At the end of the day, if disaster has struck, the ability to improvise will again depend on a company's culture, so even a large corporation may show a remarkable ability to work outside the standard band of business processes. Under no circumstances, however, should you think that breaches can be dealt with by shooting from the hip. The basis is always a defined treatment process, but people need to have the ability to think 'outside the box' to solve those problems during a breach that cannot be, or has not been anticipated.

Some companies have processes in place that allow emergency-appropriate temporary shortcuts or a business continuity setup (usually mainly for availability), which allows prompt decision making to speedily mitigate the consequences of a disaster.

**Preparedness**

The bigger companies tend to win out here, as they usually implement information security awareness programmes and have dedicated staff on their payroll. Smaller companies have a tendency to rely on ad hoc problem solving. They do not usually have processes in place to cope with an information security breach, so they need to rely on improvisation. Of course, the above only holds true if the relevant processes are actually in place, which cannot be taken for granted, even though ISO27001 has passed its

## 1: Why Risk does Not Depend on Company Size

30th year (starting as BS7799 in the late 80s). In other words, larger companies tend to have some advantages over smaller companies, provided said processes are actually in place and operational.

**Contacts with authority**

In some incidents, such as executive abductions, blackmail or larger cyber crime cases, intense contact with the authorities is necessary, to co-ordinate internal and external activities and to remain on top of the latest news and events in the case. Larger corporations usually have former investigators, or other law enforcement people, on their staff which makes contact with authorities easier. Smart smaller companies tend to look for people with an extensive law enforcement background and lots of contacts to fulfil a security function, whereas the standard small company will be disadvantaged due its lack of staff and of experience in dealing with breaches.

In summary, then, risk does not depend on company size, because:

- risk effects can be equally devastating to all sizes of company;
- a culture for treating breaches effectively and efficiently either is, or is not, present;
- cash available depends on the company's financial success, not its size;
- the level of preparedness can vary considerably between companies of similar levels.

**At the end of the day, the elements above will define how well a company can handle a breach, and whether**

*1: Why Risk does Not Depend on Company Size*

**or not it survives the breach in the short term and over a longer period.**

## CHAPTER 2: GETTING YOUR RISK PROFILE RIGHT

The best breach is, of course, the one that never happens. In order to achieve that, it is of paramount importance to get one's risk profile right and to fully and thoroughly understand the risk situation of the company. The word 'situation' includes knowledge about threats, vulnerabilities, potential damage, likelihoods, business options for treatment and acceptable losses, all under the circumstances and business environment the company operates in for all its branches, subsidiaries and locations.

We will describe two ways of understanding one's risk profile: a rather intuitive one, to serve as a starting point yielding reasonable results, and a more extensive one, including all necessary parameters to complete an industry-standard risk analysis.

Please note that ISO27001:2013 leaves the choice of risk identification methodology entirely up to you. This provides an additional degree of freedom, but, of course, the meta-criteria of this still need to be fulfilled. These[1] are:

- having risk acceptance criteria in place;
- having a risk evaluation scheme in place;
- ensuring that the method you use produces consistent, valid, and comparable results (which

---

[1] cf. ISO 27001_2013, chapter 6.1.2

implies that you shouldn't change your method monthly, or yearly, or at least not without good reason);
- ensuring that consequences of risk materialisation are defined;
- ensuring that a likelihood of occurrence is determined;
- ensuring that an overall risk level is defined;
- ensuring that your method includes a way of prioritising risks.

In the following section, we will describe the intuitive method of risk analysis and the formal model used in information security since the early inception of ISO27001. Both approaches fulfil the above criteria; apply whichever you prefer.

**Intuitive risk analysis**

The intuitive approach starts with one simple question:

*What are the events that could seriously damage my company, its information assets and their confidentiality, availability or integrity?*

Start by asking yourself this question, and take a note of your answers. Then ask your senior managers the same question, and collect and co-ordinate all the answers. At this stage, let each person work individually, maybe even anonymously.

## 2: Getting your Risk Profile Right

If you wish, you can now have these results reviewed by a consultant you trust to bring in an unbiased external view. Choose this consultant carefully, as you will expose much of your company to them (and make sure the consultant signs an NDA containing pretty stiff penalties for breaching it).

Once it has been established what these events are, take it one step further and ask the questions below for each of the events identified in the first step.

- How much damage would the company suffer from this event?
- How much damage would be acceptable for this event, for all events of the same type, and for all events per year?
- How likely is this event? Does the product of occurrences and damages exceed the acceptable level?

After answering these questions you are almost done. The final question would be:

- What is the cost of mitigation to prevent the described events from happening, and does this make sense financially in regard to the risk? Note that it might not fully make sense financially, but might still make overall sense in order, for example, to prevent a loss of reputation.

Once you have completed this step, you have not only done everything ISO27001 would like you to do in terms of risk analysis, you have also achieved a result that immediately shows which problems to tackle first, and where you could have some quick wins. You would first tackle either the situations where only a little effort is needed to significantly reduce the risk profile, or those that can be mitigated with

## 2: Getting your Risk Profile Right

little effort, but with a less significant effect on the risk profile. Make sure, however, that the impetus of mitigation activities is not lost and that all risks on the list are covered.

This type of risk analysis should be repeated:

- yearly, to make sure you stay on top of your game;
- whenever your business or infrastructure changes significantly (for example, by migrating to new technology, introducing new technology or opening a new branch in a less secure country).

**Formal risk analysis**

In formal risk analysis, it is important to use a defined way of producing comparable results, and to be transparent about those results and how you arrived at them. Of course, that transparency applies only to those who need to know about the results. Target groups could be external auditors, internal auditors, senior management asked for a decision on how to deal with risks identified, and so on.

*Step 1 – Identifying threats*

In the first step, you try to find out which risks you really need to care about. In the modern understanding of information security, this means evaluating your threats and vulnerabilities. The very first step is, therefore, actually an analysis of your company in regard to:

- physical sites and locations and their characteristics (e.g. power, number of rooms, locks, etc.);
- information assets;

## 2: Getting your Risk Profile Right

- IT infrastructure, including architecture, networks, server operating systems, software and database products used.

Once you have completed this inventory of business information assets and IT assets, it is a good idea to use the threats and vulnerabilities catalogue of the German Baseline Protection Manual. As of the beginning of 2014, this contains about 510 different threats, which you can then check against your asset inventory. The German Baseline Protection Manual is fully available online in English, and is free for public use. You can find it under *https://www.bsi.bund.de/cln_156/EN/Topics/ITGrundschutz /ITGrundschutzCatalogues/itgrundschutzcatalogues_node.h tml*. Look for the international section, which provides all information contained in English.

We will not delve deeper into it, but only mention that, as a free catalogue of threats and vulnerabilities, it has proven very valuable when performing risk analysis. It is updated about four times a year.

Step 1 of your analysis will provide you with a table of your inventory and the risks related to it. Practically speaking, it is efficient to use the manual's threat list, and enter identification tags or descriptions of your assets to which these threats apply. You could also assign traffic-light colours to threat relevance levels – we recommend using the definitions below.

- Green: generally relevant, but the mitigation measures in place are sufficient to stop the threat from becoming a risk.
- Yellow: generally relevant, and the measures taken so far do mitigate it, but not entirely, leaving room for exploitation of the associated vulnerability.

## 2: Getting your Risk Profile Right

- Red: generally relevant, and there are no mitigation measures in place, or these are not effective. The threat could therefore materialise any time, depending only on the will of the attacker to affect it.
- Grey: not relevant. It should still be listed, though, as relevance may change over time, maybe very quickly, as a result of the implementation of new technology, or to ensure that the threat is not overlooked or forgotten in the future.

A sample table is shown in Table 1.

**Notes for Table 1**

- Threat numbering and naming follows the German Baseline Protection Catalogues system.
- The 'Affects' column describes the affected assets by their ID as set up in the object catalogue (asset inventory). 'H' stands for hardware, 'N' for networking devices, 'I' for infrastructure and 'D' for assets under control of entities other than the company. You can choose the naming convention most suitable to yourself and your environment. In large organisations, you might have standard categories defined in your configuration management database (CMDB) derived from an ITIL®-related IT management process.
- In performing this first step, you will have reached a decision on whether certain threats are relevant to your enterprise and can become risks.

## 2: Getting your Risk Profile Right

**Table 1**

| Threat | Relevant | Status | Affects | Note |
|---|---|---|---|---|
| G 1.1 – Loss of personnel | ✓ | Green | IT staff | Number of employees is currently sufficient to ensure 24x7 operation (as stipulated by internal SLA). |
| G 1.2 – Failure of IT system | ✓ | Green | H.all | Sufficient degree of redundancy, coupled dependencies are low. |
| G 1.7 – Inadmissible temperature and humidity | ✓ | Yellow | H.all N.all | Preventive and detective controls exist; server room has redundant air conditioning system. Networking room has only air conditioning, but thermal load is low. |

## 2: Getting your Risk Profile Right

| Threat | Relevant | Status | Affects | Note |
|---|---|---|---|---|
| G 1.10 – Failure of a wide area network | ✓ | Red | D.5 D.7 | Internet connection is not redundant, company has no power to influence stability of line. |
| G 1.13 – Storms | ✓ | Yellow | H.all N.all | Very heavy storms could lead to parts of adjacent buildings falling and damaging company buildings. |
| G 3.6 – Hazards posed by cleaning staff or outside staff | ✓ | Red | D.all | Current regulations are not commensurate with baseline risk profile of company, due to company branch of business. |

## 2: Getting your Risk Profile Right

| Threat | Relevant | Status | Affects | Note |
|---|---|---|---|---|
| G 5.3 – Unauthorised entry into a building | ✓ | Red | I.1 | Badge carrying is reversed; only visitors wear badges. It is easy to bypass the central gate; the perimeter is not sufficiently secured. |
| G 5.4 – Theft | ✓ | Red | H.all | Theft of user PCs is possible any time; lack of awareness among gate personnel. |
| G 5.95 – Bugging of indoor conversations over mobile phones | ✓ | Red | All rooms | There is not a policy, nor are there measures in place to prevent this type of bugging. |

### *Step 2 – Assigning damage and likelihood*

Once the table of relevant threats has been established, you will need to think about the damage to your assets, and the impact that can result from the threat materialising, as well as the likelihood of it occurring at all. In information security, the term 'likelihood' has started to replace the

## 2: Getting your Risk Profile Right

term 'probability' as, for many events, no scientifically sound definition or calculation of probability can be given. According to the 'garbage-in, garbage-out' principle, it makes much more sense to think thoroughly about a number of occurrences per year than to fiddle around with complex formulae, whose input is usually flawed, and which are certainly not precise enough to yield a significant, sound result. Sometimes, the more complex the formula, the less truth it bears.

When assessing damage, you should consider single damage, e.g. an IT centre being flooded and the cost of replacing the equipment (straightforward to calculate), as well as damage propagating through a business process (downstream effects). As an absolute minimum, consider penalties due to customers, should you be unable to render your services as contractually agreed. You might also want to factor in:

- internal cost of overtime to deal with an event;
- cost of people not working when they should, but cannot, due to an event;
- cost of temporary staff and consultants hired to deal with an event;
- accumulating damages in production cycles or a value chain (downstream effects);
- cost of temporary equipment, transportation, and lease of materials (e.g. IT equipment) for the duration of an event.

In this step you estimate or calculate likelihoods and damages for every threat as best you can, and multiply the damage by the likelihood. This will yield the Annual Loss Expectancy for the individual threats, which have now become risks due to this added information.

## 2: Getting your Risk Profile Right

Your table could now look as shown in Table 2, below.

**Notes on Table 2**

- Likelihood is stated as number of occurrences per year, so once a year would yield 1, once every two years would yield 0.5, and once a month would yield 12.
- Including occurrence figures less than 1 makes sense only to remind you that there is a risk that can materialise in general, but will not materialise on a regular annual basis. Including its associated damage based on an occurrence of less than once a year is a way of justifying investments needed to protect against this particular risk on a yearly basis (as companies usually define yearly budgets, not budgets that extend over longer periods).
- For threats 3.6, 5.3 and 5.95 it is quite clear that such acts could result in a loss of business, therefore the damage has been assumed to be equivalent to the average value of a project for this sample company.
- Threat 5.4 assumes that all laptops are encrypted, so damage would be reduced to the value of the physical device, which is assumed as being a little higher than usual.

## 2: Getting your Risk Profile Right

**Table 2**

| Threat | Likelihood | Damage | ALE | Note |
|---|---|---|---|---|
| G 1.1 – Loss of personnel | 0.33 | 70,000 | 23,100 | Assumed to happen once every three years. |
| G 1.2 – Failure of IT system | 0.1 | 5 million | 500,000 | Assumed to happen once every ten years; figure includes subsequent damage. |
| G 1.7 – Inadmissible temperature and humidity | 12 | 0 | 0 | Assumed to happen once a month, but no impact, due to high level of redundancy and low thermal load. |
| G 1.10 – Failure of a wide area network | 2 | 50,000 | 100,000 | Assumed to happen twice a year; damage is calculated by adding up lost hours. |

## 2: Getting your Risk Profile Right

| Threat | Likelihood | Damage | ALE | Note |
|---|---|---|---|---|
| G 1.13 – Storms | 0.01 | 10 million | 100,000 | Assumed to happen once every 100 years; figure is estimate only, and includes damage to buildings and re-establishment of facilities. |
| G 3.6 – Hazards posed by cleaning staff or outside staff | 1 | 220 million | 220 million | Could happen any time; intruders could take away sensitive documents leading to lost bids; figure is based on typical project revenue. |
| G 5.3 – Unauthorised entry into a building | 1 | 220 million | 220 million | Bound to happen, same effect as for G 3.6. |
| G 5.4 – Theft | 0.5 | 5,000 | 2,500 | Assumed to happen once every two years; only an end-user PC or laptop affected. |
| G 5.95 – Bugging of indoor conversations over mobile phones | 1 | 220 million | 220 million | Bound to happen; same effect as for G 3.6. |

## 2: Getting your Risk Profile Right

### Step 3 – Defining acceptable loss

This is a separate step from those above because, if you separate the steps distinctly, you will get a better result, unbiased by your own concepts of what is affordable or not. What you do is add a figure, a limit, of what would constitute acceptable loss per year for that risk, and for all risks in total. That figure should be aligned with one of the following items. Bear in mind that the cost of an incident or breach has to be financed somehow; the money has to come from somewhere. Potential sources of finance are:

- cash reserves (short-term cash, in accounting terms)
- revenue (percentage of revenue)
- profit (percentage of profit)

We would recommend using cash reserves as a basis, as this is money that is readily available. Percentages of revenue or profit may not mean much if revenue or profits decline suddenly or unexpectedly, either before the breach, because of a general deterioration of the business situation, or due to the breach itself.

You would, therefore, assign a figure of acceptable loss to each risk, and assign a percentage of cash reserves to the total ALE, not to exceed, for example, 10% of reserves. You may wish to align your damage levels with that and consider all potential damages that would consume more than 25% of reserves, for instance, as 'substantial'.

Once you have completed Step 3, you are basically done, as you have arrived at a table of risks sorted by relevance. It makes sense, though, to take the analysis one step further and consider mitigation costs in a separate step. That will enable you to prioritise risks and their associated mitigation measures based on your ability to do something about it. No

## 2: Getting your Risk Profile Right

external auditor could take offence with such a procedure; in fact they would completely approve of it. Table 3 shows Table 2 with added Acceptable Loss (AL) information.

### Table 3

| Threat | Likelihood | Damage | ALE | AL |
|---|---|---|---|---|
| G 1.1 – Loss of personnel | 0.33 | 70,000 | 23,100 | 30,000 |
| G 1.2 – Failure of IT system | 0.1 | 5 million | 500,000 | 1,000 |
| G 1.7 – Inadmissible temperature and humidity | 12 | 0 | 0 | 0 |
| G 1.10 – Failure of a wide area network | 2 | 50,000 | 100,000 | 0 |
| G 1.13 – Storms | 0.01 | 10 million | 100,000 | 100,000 |
| G 3.6 – Hazards posed by cleaning staff or outside staff | 1 | 220 million | 220 million | 0 |

## 2: Getting your Risk Profile Right

| Threat | Likelihood | Damage | ALE | AL |
|---|---|---|---|---|
| G 5.3 – Unauthorised entry into a building | 1 | 220 million | 220 million | 0 |
| G 5.4 – Theft | 0.5 | 5,000 | 2,500 | 20,000 |
| G 5.95 – Bugging of indoor conversations over mobile phones | 1 | 220 million | 220 million | 0 |

As you can see from Table 3, the company will accept a yearly amount for replacing personnel which is higher than the ALE shows. This means that the threat or risk can be accepted.

The ALE figure for failure of the IT system is actually higher than allowed which, in this step, means that the company must act on this risk.

The table also shows that the anticipated loss from lost contracts is totally unacceptable which, again, points to a need for action in regard to threats 3.6, 5.3 and 5.95.

Table 4 now shows Table 3 with some added action priority information, based on a measure of how acceptable each risk is. The measure of 'how acceptable' is actually established by the difference between ALE and Acceptable Loss (AL); the higher the difference, the higher the priority.

## 2: Getting your Risk Profile Right

### Table 4

| Priority | Threat | Likeli-hood | Damage | ALE | AL |
|---|---|---|---|---|---|
| 1 | G 3.6 – Hazards posed by cleaning staff or outside staff | 1 | 220 million | 220 million | 0 |
| 1 | G 5.3 – Unauthorised entry into a building | 1 | 220 million | 220 million | 0 |
| 1 | G 5.95 – Bugging of indoor conversations over mobile phones | 1 | 220 million | 220 million | 0 |
| 4 | G 1.10 – Failure of a wide area network | 2 | 50,000 | 100,000 | 0 |
| 5 | G 1.2 – Failure of IT system | 0.1 | 5 million | 5 million | 100,000 |
| 6 | G 1.13 – Storms | 0.01 | 10 million | 100,000 | 100,000 |

## 2: Getting your Risk Profile Right

| Priority | Threat | Likeli-hood | Damage | ALE | AL |
|---|---|---|---|---|---|
| 7 | G 1.7 – Inadmissible temperature and humidity | 12 | 0 | 0 | 0 |
| 8 | G 1.1 – Loss of personnel | 0.33 | 70,000 | 23,100 | 30,000 |
| 9 | G 5.4 – Theft | 0,5 | 5,000 | 2,500 | 20,000 |

Based on the evaluations contained in Table 3, it is clear that threats 3.6, 5.3 and 5.95 need to be treated fast, and with the same priority. They are, therefore, the top three of Table 4. The rest of the entries are sorted by the difference between ALE and AL.

The sorting is strictly mathematical with one slight difference. If a result of zero is obtained by two non-zero values of ALE and AL, then this risk will be listed before a risk whose calculation result is based on two values of zero, because the first type of risk is clearly more relevant in practical terms, as an ALE is associated with it.

### Step 4 – Defining mitigation priorities (business priorities)

Once you know about your risks and their relevance, you should think about the cost of mitigation for each risk. In the resulting table you would then immediately recognise:

## 2: Getting your Risk Profile Right

- those risks that can be mitigated with little effort;
- those risks where a little effort will have a big impact;
- risks that need some, or substantial, effort;
- risks that you will not be able to mitigate for lack of resources.

Based on these elements, you can make a sound, well-founded decision on whether to reduce or accept (or transfer) a risk. Please note that risk transfer is, in general, not a good choice. For instance, an insurance company may compensate you for a loss, but usually much later than needed, and the loss has still occurred. In other words, risk transfer does not usually work at all, and it certainly does not work well for information security risks.

*Table 5* shows the results of Table 4, with an added column on the moneys needed to mitigate the risk. It also contains a brief explanation of the mitigation measures used. Mitigation cost may be estimated, or based on offers from suppliers. We assume that all mitigation measures described reduce the ALE to zero or, at least, to the acceptable level defined.

For threat 3.6, we assume that some initial consulting may be required to set up a good policy, and that there will be running costs in regard to background checks, procurement of badges, and so on.

For threat 5.3, the initial cost is quite high, as we assume that a new gate has to be built, including a man-trap, and that running costs will be low as only badges need to be bought throughout the year.

For threat 5.95, we assume there to be no running cost, as the retrofitting of a meeting room with a Faraday cage solution, to eliminate all electromagnetic signalling, is quite

## 2: Getting your Risk Profile Right

costly (up to £70,000 per room), but has to be carried out only once per room.

For threat 1.10, we assume that there is some cost involved in establishing redundant ISP links, with quite a large amount to be spent on monthly fees.

For threat 1.2, we assume that a lot of one-time investment is needed to add even more redundancy, bringing with it elevated running costs due, in part, to higher power consumption. The figures also show that one-time mitigation cost exceeds the AL and would therefore amortise within about four years, reducing the ALE to zero right from the start. In this particular case, it would be justifiable to look into other options that offer a better cost to AL ratio.

Threat 1.13 is a good real-life example, as it shows that the mitigation cost for this particular risk heavily exceeds Acceptable Loss, rendering implementation of the measure pointless.

Threats 1.7, 1.1, and 5.4 do not require mitigation.

## 2: Getting your Risk Profile Right

Table 5

| Priority | Threat | ALE | AL | Mitigation cost initial | Mitigation cost p.a. | Mitigation measure |
|---|---|---|---|---|---|---|
| 1 | G 3.6 – Hazards posed by cleaning staff or outside staff | 220 million | 0 | 10,000 | 30,000 | Establish policy and associated measures (background checks, regular screening). |
| 1 | G 5.3 – Unauthorised entry into a building | 220 million | 0 | 70,000 | 1,000 | Build new gate and introduce badges. |
| 1 | G 5.95 – Bugging of indoor conversations over mobile phones | 220 million | 0 | 350,000 | 0 | Refit meeting rooms with a Faraday cage solution. |

## 2: Getting your Risk Profile Right

Table 5 continued

| Priority | Threat | ALE | AL | Mitigation cost initial | Mitigation cost p.a. | Mitigation measure |
|---|---|---|---|---|---|---|
| 4 | G 1.10 – Failure of a WAN | 100,000 | 0 | 15,000 | 60,000 | Establish redundant ISP links. |
| 5 | G 1.2 – Failure of IT system | 500,000 | 100,000 | 350,000 | 30,000 | Add even more redundancy: running cost includes added power. |
| 6 | G 1.13 – Storms | 100.000 | 100,000 | 10 million | 0 | Relocate factory. |
| 7 | G 1.7 – Inadmissible temperature and humidity | 0 | 0 | | | No mitigation needed. |
| 8 | G 1.1 – Loss of personnel | 23,100 | 30,000 | | | No mitigation needed. |
| 9 | G 5.4 – Theft | 2,500 | 20,000 | | | No mitigation needed. |

## 2: Getting your Risk Profile Right

Table 5 can now be reduced to contain only relevant risks. The next step is to sort these risks.

- Low cost, high impact mitigation measures come first.
- Medium to high cost, high impact mitigation measures come next.
- All others follow in order of ascending cost-to-impact ratio.
- Exceptions can be allowed if, by equal rank, the potential damage of one risk is significantly higher than that of another, thereby putting an emphasis on potentially doubtful cases.

This gives us Table 6, below, our final prioritised result.

With the risks chosen for this sample company, the problem remains that the first three risks are equal in their devastating effect, but, based on our rules, 5.95 comes before 1.10 as the cost to impact ratio is much lower than for 1.10 (as ALE would drop to zero in all cases, but the amount of the drop is less for 1.10 than for 5.95). Remember to look at the ratio, not only at the cost figure.

If you look closely at the final result, you will notice that the result is well structured and makes a lot of sense in practical terms. First, we deal with the gate, then with better choosing and checking on cleaning and other non-company personnel, then we take care of bugging, deal with the WAN and, finally, improve the IT system. One could argue that bugging should be treated before the staff issue, and in real life you have, of course, the power to choose to do so.

## 2: Getting your Risk Profile Right

Table 6

| Priority | Threat | ALE | AL | Mitigation cost initial | Mitigation cost p.a. | Mitigation cost over 3 years | Mitigation measure |
|---|---|---|---|---|---|---|---|
| 1 | G 5.3 – Unauthorised entry into a building | 220 million | 0 | 70,000 | 1,000 | 73,000 | Build new gate and introduce badges. |
| 2 | G 3.6 – Hazards posed by cleaning staff or outside staff | 220 million | 0 | 10,000 | 30,000 | 100,000 | Establish policy and associated measures (background checks, regular screening). |

## 2: Getting your Risk Profile Right

**Table 6 continued**

| | | | | | | |
|---|---|---|---|---|---|---|
| 3 | G 5.95 – Bugging of indoor conversations over mobile phones | 220 million | 0 | 350,000 | 0 | 350,000 | Refit meeting rooms with a Faraday cage solution. |
| 4 | G 1.10 – Failure of a WAN | 100,000 | 0 | 15,000 | 60,000 | 195,000 | Establish redundant ISP links. |
| 5 | G 1.2 – Failure of IT system | 500,000 | 100,000 | 350,000 | 30,000 | 440,000 | Add even more redundancy; running cost includes added power. |

## 2: Getting your Risk Profile Right

On a practical note, you can expect a full risk analysis, as outlined here, to be completed in one week for small- to medium-sized infrastructures with no more than 200 elements, and up to three months for the initial effort for larger enterprises. You may wish to conduct the analysis for selected business processes only, but, if you do so, be aware of the interfaces between these processes and others, so that damage effects and propagation can be calculated correctly and truthfully.

Every risk analysis should be checked for accuracy about once a year, and they may need more frequent updates if technology, assets or infrastructure change significantly. It is safe to define 'significantly' as 'Yes, it has an impact on the risk profile at first sight'.

**Residual risks**

Once you have worked your way through the process of identifying and subsequently mitigating risks as best you can, as well as available resources allow, or according to the established priorities through the risk identification process, those risks that still remain open or which have not been fully mitigated remain in your risk profile as so-called residual risks. In other words, think of the mitigation measures that you identified and implemented as filters through which you have run your risks. Your risk profile has now been clarified through filtering, with only those risks remaining about which nothing can be done, or which still retain some degree of risk exposure (this degree being significantly reduced compared with how it was before mitigation took place).

## 2: Getting your Risk Profile Right

These residual risks need to be addressed in business continuity and disaster recovery plans. People often only consider natural disasters when thinking about residual risks. In order not to limit the scope and nature of residual risks contained in business continuity plans, you may wish to call such a plan 'Residual Risk Treatment Plan', by which term you will express that you consider all residual risks, and do not impose intellectual censorship on your risk profile.

Please note that there is a distinct difference between a business continuity plan and an IT service continuity plan. The former deals with how to keep the essential revenue generation process (sales process) up and running, or to bring it back to functioning, while the latter deals only with getting required IT services back into an operational state.

Let's consider the following example to illustrate the difference between business and IT service continuity.

If your company's mail system suffers a severe functional breach and needs to be taken offline, or even no longer exists (maybe due to a physical attack), the main function to restore is to be able to send and receive e-mail. This can be achieved independently of the specific product used and, while users may, for some time, not have all those handy and comfortable functions that they are used to, any replacement system that can send and deliver mail will help to re-establish the e-mail function. So, for instance, it is possible to replace a Microsoft Exchange-based solution with a temporary Linux solution, as the latter will be very straightforward and easy to set up in case of a disaster. The purpose of a temporary solution is to be temporary, however, and you would either draft a plan to get the full service back online at a particular time after the disaster, or

## 2: Getting your Risk Profile Right

you would actually have your business continuity plan (BCP) include a section describing how the same functionality (Microsoft® Exchange) can be brought up on a different hardware platform.

If your company is an industrial company and one of your plants burns down, the IT contained there is not your first priority. The first priority (apart from saving lives) is how to:

- move production to another site, thereby keeping up output;
- buy, from another company, the goods that can no longer be produced in this situation;
- find another way to cope with the damage.

# CHAPTER 3: WHAT IS A BREACH?

Defining what constitutes a breach of information is not easy. Does only criminal activity constitute a breach? Is it only the things we read and hear about in the media (such as the army 'losing' data), or does everything that causes damage count as a breach? These are practical questions, even though they may sound strange at first.

When establishing the roles, responsibilities, processes and technologies required in a company to ensure information security, these questions can be answered with ease at the technical level. They start to become more complex once the differing views of affected departments come to light; and the situation is aggravated when the parties involved lose focus and start playing politics instead of trying to solve the issues at hand. The bigger the company, the more likely this is to happen.

It is therefore important to provide a definition, or a working set of definitions, for use as the basis for consensus in a company.

The term 'breach' is not actually defined in the ISO27000 family. What is defined, though, is the term 'incident', as:

*Information security incident*[2]

*[A] single or a series of unwanted or unexpected information security events that have a significant probability of compromising business operations and threatening information security.*

---

[2] cf. ISO27000:2012, Terms and Definitions, 2.32.

## 3: What is a Breach?

Let us look in more detail at some of the phrases in this definition.

### *A single or a series...*

The Standard acknowledges that, when something adverse happens, one single incident can be as damaging as a series of events.

The Standard does not provide guidance in regard to the number of incidents or the timeframe in which they occur. You need to establish this yourself, ensuring that your company's specific requirements are met. The larger the company, the easier it will be to set up a formal regime of timeline and number thresholds. Ideally, you would set up a classification scheme which would provide an answer based on the number, timeframe and expected severity of the event.

### *...significant probability of compromising ...*

Do not be fooled – probability does not help in an adverse situation. Probability and statistics as a whole tend to be unsuitable tools for incident-related business decisions. You need to assess the impact of the event on your business operations. To do this, you will need to review technical and business processes, contracts and maybe criminal and civil law, as well as external factors, such as the public's reaction, media coverage, and so on.

Using the word 'probability' about an incident does not make much sense, as it suggests that there is a level at which no harm is done at all. Furthermore, it tends to provide a false sense of security. Instead, a thorough and dispassionate evaluation and the results of your incident-related deliberations are far more likely to give you an accurate picture of the situation.

## 3: What is a Breach?

To clarify matters, and as a starting point, let us briefly consider what constitutes information security. According to ISO27001, information security consists of ensuring the *confidentiality*, the *availability* and the *integrity* of information, as well as any other pillars that the company has decided to include, such as *non-repudiation*.

This means that any event which adversely affects the level of service of the processes charged with preserving confidentiality, availability or integrity (or whatever other pillars have been chosen) should be considered a breach. This is a good first thought when establishing the processes dealing with incident handling for your information security management system (ISMS).

In detail, a breach can be defined as a breach of:

- confidentiality
- availability
- integrity

**Confidentiality breach**

A breach of confidentiality occurs every time the need-to-know principle, on which all dissemination of information should be based, is violated. Please note that the breach does not occur when the damage becomes visible, it occurs at the point in time when the company's guidelines have been violated. This difference is important, as it illustrates that the true point in time of a breach may be hard to determine, since a breach can take place in writing using a covert channel, by oral transmission or by electronic means including eavesdropping.

# 3: What is a Breach?

**Availability breach**

A breach of availability can occur when the availability of your IT systems and the business services using them is reduced due to an adverse event (for example, millions of spam mails blocking your mail server(s), or a virus spreading throughout a network and rendering client PCs or even servers unusable); or when the Service Level Agreements (SLAs) that are in place are not adhered to, quite independently of any actual damage that may, or may not, result.

The latter point is a rather formal argument, based on the literal meaning of the word 'breach'. While it is normal to use the term for incidents affecting confidentiality and leading to unwanted disclosure of information, temporary unavailability of systems or services is not normally defined as a breach. People prefer to call this an 'incident' (based on terms used in the ITIL® framework).

What does happen, though, as described above, is that a security breach materialises and affects the availability of systems and services adversely up to a complete (but usually temporary) standstill. Depending on the degree to which the business services rely on the availability of IT systems (for example, hospitals, industrial plants, mobile telephony providers and Internet service providers), such situations can be treated as breaches. At the same time, some work will have to be carried out to determine whether the root cause of the incident was a security breach or 'just' some functional failure. In the context of this book, we focus only on availability problems that resulted from security breaches or security incidents.

# 3: What is a Breach?

## Integrity breach

An integrity breach occurs whenever the integrity of information or its means of storage are violated, for example, by transmission errors, by intentional manipulation, by unintentional handling errors or by the corruption of file content or structure due to electrical, magnetic or other failures.

These definitions are quite broad, however, and include everyone and everything, so they need to be narrowed down for practical purposes. As a next step, you should establish that a breach has three dimensions of characteristics which jointly incorporate all the aspects required for treatment. These are:

- impact
- source
- general treatment options

### *Impact*

Impact deals with what the incident is capable of causing. Will it only affect the company in a minor way (perhaps a server outage of not more than five minutes) or will it cause irreparable damage to the operations and the reputation of the company? Or will its effect be somewhere between the two? Can it affect the stock price of the company?

You need to set up a clear, non-overlapping set of levels of impact that should be aligned to:

- purely financial impact
- reputational impact – world
- reputational impact – customers
- legal impact

## 3: What is a Breach?

It is important to make these distinctions, as these categories are not necessarily connected and can materialise alone or jointly.

A purely financial impact would result from an incident where money alone is sufficient as a remedy, such as a defective power supply that caused a server outage.

The difference between 'reputational impact – world' and 'reputational impact – customers' is made because these two target groups are not necessarily connected, and communication with these groups usually differs in many aspects.

Take the defence sector, for example. It does not communicate with the public by banners in football stadiums or large advert campaigns, and its business is independent of the public mood.

On the other hand, insurance or tobacco companies and online betting sites communicate heavily with the general public which is their customer base.

A known breach of information security would, therefore, have a different effect on the remedial actions required by each of these sectors.

A legal impact results from the risk of being sued, or of having to sue to recover damages. This risk needs to be split into those legal risks directly affecting the company, and risks applying to people (for example, in the case of an executive director's wrongdoing). Ultimately, legal risks imply financial risks, but, at an individual level, they also include having to serve time in prison.

# 3: What is a Breach?

## Source

What you can do about an incident heavily depends on where, what and who the source is. Incidents can have multiple sources (as used in this paragraph) and sometimes the source (or 'root cause' as the ISO9000 community would call it) will only come to light after thorough investigation.

Potential source categories to consider are:

- external vs. internal
- unintentional vs. intentional
- manual vs. automatic
- human vs. nature

*External vs. internal*

*External* refers to all sources which are not part of the company. *Internal* refers only to employees (those with a contract of employment) whereas all others, including freelancers, quasi-permanent freelancers, temporary workers, other companies, customers and suppliers are external. The difference is important, as the means of incident management are distinctly different. An employee can easily be interviewed about his role in an incident, while it might not be so easy in the case of externals or contractors, who might simply refuse solely on legal grounds.

To a certain extent, it is odd that externals can usually be made to co-operate more easily than employees, while employees actually have stricter contracts in terms of general labour law. In most countries, labour law requires the employee to demonstrate a level of trustworthiness

## 3: What is a Breach?

which is not required by general business partners. Indeed, based solely on common law, a business contract cannot usually be terminated on the grounds of a lack of trustworthiness, which is why this is explicitly included in some co-operation contracts.

The bottom line is that the points below will decide the chances of success, should force or pressure be required to ensure co-operation in solving a case.

- The level of dependency on the business relationship or employment.
- The number of people involved, independent of whether the breach was of a criminal nature or the result of negligence or lack of training. The higher the number here, the more difficult it will be to crack the 'network'.
- The options that you can provide to the human source to come forward with the truth. A human with a lot to lose will, quite naturally, try to avoid co-operation, to destroy evidence and to resist interviews until there is no alternative.

*Unintentional vs. intentional*

*Unintentional* incidents usually point to one of the following:

**A lack of training.** This should be immediately remedied by appropriate training, and is one of the cases where an unwillingness to spend money up front (by providing the training in the first place) can have a disproportionately negative effect.

## 3: What is a Breach?

**A lack of experience.** This makes it necessary to replace the employee or employees at fault with more experienced ones.

**A process irregularity.** The process must be made clearer, easier to understand, or generally more accessible.

**Technical deficiency of a software product.** Changes must be made to the product's human interface or its deeper technical characteristics. You need to ensure that, especially when it comes to critical infrastructures, the systems should allow easy human interaction otherwise they will be risk prone.

*Intentional* incidents, however, usually occur simply because someone found that the results of the incident improved their life, or provided some worthwhile advantage. This applies equally to the banker who steals millions from customer accounts, to the teenager who tries to sell company data for a quick buck, or to the spy who steals data for his/her government's use, as well as to politically motivated hackers who want to express an opinion by bringing down websites containing views to which they are opposed.

A proactive program to prevent incidents from occurring should ask the questions below.

- What is our level of exposure to malevolent groups of people?
- Who may want to harm us?

The usual suspects include disgruntled employees, greedy high- and medium-level managers, and employees who are short of cash.

- How would they try to harm us?

## 3: What is a Breach?

For example, by denial of service attacks, by trying to damage our reputation or by bribery.

Developing answers to these questions best suited to your company and its specific market situation will greatly help you to decide on the specific measures you need to implement.

### Manual vs. automatic

If the source of a breach was *manual* action, then the way to prevent the same breach from happening again may differ from a situation where the source of the breach resulted from a malfunction of an *automatic* process. In the latter case, the breach will result in changes to the system, be it a process or a specific software program whereas, in the manual case, it may be advisable to replace manual process steps with automatic ones, or to strengthen training.

### Human vs. nature

The recurrence of breaches and incidents, whose root cause was *human* actions, can be prevented by replacing the human element with a computerised version of the same task, or by improving the training provided to the human in carrying out the task that caused the breach. Where the breach was intentional, of course, removing the human entirely from the situation is the more effective remedy.

If *nature* was to blame for the incident, such as a flood, an earthquake or a lightning strike, preventing the same type of incident from recurring tends to be much harder and more costly. In the case of floods, for example, flood gates

## 3: What is a Breach?

might not be enough – you might have to relocate the entire company.

### General treatment options

These are covered in detail in Chapter 4, in the section entitled *Dimensions of treatment / mitigation of information security breaches*.

## CHAPTER 4: GENERAL AVOIDANCE AND MITIGATION STRATEGIES

### Introduction – general aspects, avoidance and related ISO27001 controls

As already mentioned, this book deals only with severe incidents, referred to as 'breaches' and with breaches in the strict sense of the word, meaning that damage to *confidentiality*, *availability* or *integrity* of information has actually occurred, or is bound to occur, if mitigation of a risk does not set in immediately. In the case studies, we will mainly describe severe breaches of confidentiality (most common), followed by availability problems of such magnitude that one could call these breaches, and then just a few integrity breaches. Breaches of integrity are not so common when sticking close to our definition, as the intentional manipulation of data is usually more of a sideline activity within a greater confidentiality breach (for instance, manipulating a log file as a way to hide the actual unauthorised access to information and data). Causing an integrity breach by itself, such as through a distributed denial-of-service (DDoS) attack, would rather be classed as cyber warfare.

General avoidance of breaches rests on three pillars:

- people
- processes
- technology

This implies that you need to train staff, you need to have processes in place or to add security elements to existing

## 4: General Avoidance and Mitigation Strategies

business and IT processes, and you need to use some sort of technology to prevent or detect breaches.

Implementing ISO27001 can, of course, be seen as a major strategy for the avoidance of breaches, since that is what ISO27001 is about. In fact, if you implemented all 114 controls in sufficient detail for your risk profile, you would have done a pretty good job, as the 'three pillars' mentioned above are fully contained in the Standard, particularly the process and people dimensions. ISO27001 will not ask you to implement specific products, but the technical chapters of the Standard deal with functionality requirements, which you can then implement as you see fit.

**People**

The people dimension has three main elements:

- ethics
- training
- obligations

The ethics element relates to promoting an ethical environment within your company, starting at the top and promoting (sometimes enforcing) this throughout the company.

The training element refers to training your people in information security, in recognising and denying social engineering, and in the technical security skills needed.

The obligations element refers to having rules in place that transparently regulate disciplinary action, and establish duties in regard to the safeguarding of information and appropriate behaviour when a breach is detected. As a minimum, non-disclosure agreements (NDAs) need to be

## 4: General Avoidance and Mitigation Strategies

established, and security obligations should be included in employment contracts. If this last means changing existing contracts, it will need careful handling, helping people to understand the reasons behind the changes. The use of force is not a good idea here, as it may instil grudges in people and actually raise your risk profile instead of lowering it.

Remember that the 'people' category includes not only your employees, consultants and temporary workers, but also your suppliers and customers – in short, all stakeholders. Sometimes you may find it harder to educate the board of directors or the supervisory board than to educate employees, but all stakeholders should nevertheless be included in an appropriate way that draws them 'into the boat' instead of alienating them.

ISO27001 offers several controls dealing with security requirements related to people. There are direct ones, as contained in the chapter entitled *Human Resource Security*, and indirect ones that deal with organisational issues, or other subjects where people are heavily involved.

We will discuss all of these in the following pages, starting with those directly related to people. These are included in Chapter 7 of the Standard, which is divided into three parts. 7.1 deals with controls affecting employment, 7.2 deals with controls being applied during employment, while 7.3 deals with controls applied to termination or change of employment.

### *A.7.1.1 – Screening*

This control states that background verification checks on all candidates for a job shall be carried out aligned with the risk profile of the job and in accordance with local laws and

## 4: General Avoidance and Mitigation Strategies

ethics; the author strongly agrees with this. You may find, however, that your actual ability to carry out a thorough or, at least, well-founded background check will be subjected to very different legal constraints depending on country or local legislation. The panacea for this situation is to have the candidate sign that all information provided is true, and that providing false information has been agreed between you (the employer) and the candidate as being grounds for immediate dismissal. Note that some employment laws in western Europe will allow an employee to lie about certain, defined, things to his/her employer, e.g. women are, generally, allowed to lie about if they are pregnant or not at the time of start of employment. While this particular example is rather not security relevant, take care and consult with your legal department about such situations in which a lie in response to a questionnaire might be allowed. Generally, though, this way, at least you can add a layer of protection, enabling a fast solution, should the employee be found out later to have provided false information. This will certainly hold true for lies about prior positions, certifications, prior convictions, etc. This control requires that you stay explicitly within the framework of the law, applicable regulations and ethics. Furthermore, the intensity of the background check must be proportional to the business requirements, the classification of the information to be handled and the risk profile of the job.

On a practical note, a background check can cost as little as £1,000 or more than £30,000, depending on how extensive it is.

Furthermore, you should be aware of the risk groups below.

- Cleaning personnel. They usually have access to all areas, and therefore need to be carefully selected and

## 4: General Avoidance and Mitigation Strategies

supervised, or even monitored. Some companies will even directly employ their cleaning personnel (rather than employing them through an agency) to ensure that they feel sufficiently 'welcome', can be regulated by direct action (which is a plus), and do not deviate into a path of stealing confidential information.

- Third-party service/consulting providers with a high turn-over of personnel. While a high turn-over by itself is a sign of a lack of management culture, the effect for you, as the customer, is that people change frequently and that screening large numbers of people might not be cost effective.
- External auditors. These are usually people that you cannot select, so you have no knowledge about their background and their aspirations. Even so, they become familiar with most or all of your company's intimate details. We tend to rely on ethical rules to cover this particular situation, but you should also enforce the signing of NDAs, and agree hefty penalties if your company's information security suffers a breach, whether intentional or through their negligence.
- People with CVs that look too good to be true. These usually really are too good to be true, and some deeper inspection may be required.
- People who display an overly arrogant attitude. If you are not looking for exactly this kind of person, you may find that the CV has been altered to look better, and the attitude on display is a cover for this deception.

*Methods of screening*

Let us look at the methods that can be used for screening.

## 4: General Avoidance and Mitigation Strategies

**References**. When using references, ensure that they give a balanced view. Former employers may not be the best source, as activities in that particular employment may not be relevant to the current situation. Try to get multiple sources for references and, when in doubt, do not hesitate to ask the candidate directly about facts you are unsure of.

**Criminal records**. These will only be significant if you notice that the candidate has a relevant conviction, for instance for fraud. Be aware that our daily negligence in driving can quite easily mean that somebody ends up with a conviction for involuntary manslaughter, while still being the perfect fit for the job. You should, of course, be very suspicious if you find a conviction related to the field of work. In such a case, it is generally safer to distrust than to trust.

**Full intelligence check**. This is offered in some countries, performed by the authorities, including a full check of public and non-public records. Once again, though, in some countries this may be a formal process following a legal protocol, with the subject of the check having the right to contest the result. This may end up in court, or even create some liability on your part, for denying a job based on negligently gathered information.

**Background check** by a professional investigator. For jobs comprising a high risk profile, you should consider hiring a professional investigator, as they will go to great lengths to produce verifiable and valid results. There is also the additional benefit that they are able to acquire information which is otherwise inaccessible. Treat this type of information with care as, while it may be absolutely truthful, the potential to verify it is limited. You will know a good professional investigator by the quality of their

## 4: General Avoidance and Mitigation Strategies

contacts, how discreet they are and the transparency of services offered.

### A.7.1.2 – Terms and conditions of employment

Control 7.1.2 states that contractual agreements with employees (and contractors, don't forget about contractors!) shall state their (and their organization's) responsibilities for information security. This has three major implications:

1. The responsibility for information security

    The contract should state as explicitly as possible which responsibilities regarding information security exist. This might be through a reference to the company's information security policy or by explicitly stating specific responsibilities. Usually, the first variant is chosen and you may choose to have the future employee sign the security policy as part of the document package he/she receives when employment start.

2. The job description

    It is, of course, usual today to keep an employment contract rather abstract and to state all specifics of the job (tasks, objectives, bonus regulations, etc.) in a job description. Hence, this job description should contain all those explicitly stated information security requirements the employee is obliged to follow as part of his specific job. Try to include only those requirements in the job description that are specific to the job; all others that may exist in the company, but that are not specific to that particular job will, most likely, be summarized in a number of policies, at least an Acceptable Use Policy, which

## 4: General Avoidance and Mitigation Strategies

will state generally acceptable and unacceptable use of assets in your particular company. Again, the job description (or the contract) can reference your information security framework or specific documents therein.

3. Transferring obligations and duties to a $3^{rd}$ party or a subcontractor

   In larger companies it is usual that an employee is actually the employee of a service provider, but works on your premises and can generally not be distinguished from other employees (apart from the colour of their badge, maybe). When looking at the contractual relationship between your company and the company you subcontracted to and who transfers this employee to work with you for some time, it is paramount that you require this company to transfer all your own requirements to their employees. Otherwise, these obligations will not exist on a legal level and you would not be able to take action according to your policies against such a subcontracted employees as the underlying requirements were simply not transferred.

When defining security roles and responsibilities these should be stated explicitly and unambiguously. The requirement includes employees, contractors and any third-party users. Furthermore, the requirements should not only be defined, but, of course, documented. The roles and specific requirements mentioned should be aligned with the information security policy of the company.

## 4: General Avoidance and Mitigation Strategies

In regard to actual security responsibilities, there are two dimensions to this control. First, larger companies will have dedicated security staff or teams. For these people, their security roles and job descriptions are quite the same thing, but utmost care needs to be given so that all powers are correctly understood, even more so by other employees who might be the subject of the security team's scrutiny.

As an example of this, company X has an extensive security department consisting of three groups, an operations group that operates security monitoring systems and offers internal consulting to IT staff; an audit group which performs source code audits (the company produces programming software for Web applications); and a management group that deals with all the business aspects of information security.

Whenever the IT networking team wants to change a firewall rule, approval is needed from the operations group. In this case, the roles are very clear and follow the four-eyes principle – the networking team will propose a change and the operational security team will allow or refuse it, or mandate an alteration to the proposed change.

The operational team will also help other IT teams to identify and mitigate information security risks arising from all kinds of IT activity, for instance, security requirements when establishing a new data centre.

Whenever a new piece of software is finished, the audit team will perform a full source code audit and may actually prevent the code from 'going live', i.e. being used on a production system.

The security management team, as opposed to the others, focuses more on internal consulting, by analysing and

## 4: General Avoidance and Mitigation Strategies

designing the security elements of business processes; this team rarely has any power over other departments except when they can produce a more powerful argument in a particular discussion.

So, the roles and responsibilities of the three security teams mentioned are quite clear, as are the limits of their power.

The second dimension relates to the security roles and responsibilities of ordinary employees, a number of which are usually summarised in an 'acceptable use policy'. This states everything an employee (or user, as this might affect temporary workers of all sorts as well) is, and is not, allowed to do with company IT resources. Sometimes the acceptable use policy will also be very specific about security requirements, such as not using unencrypted USB sticks or keeping virus protection on company laptops up to date.

As general advice, whatever you call the document should include everything that you expect a user to adhere to in terms of security requirements. This will also serve as a practical guideline to users, who can look up what they are supposed to do. Examples of content include:

- locking screens when leaving the workplace;
- observing data classification and associated handling requirements;
- observing data protection requirements, which should be stated in detail;
- contacts among security staff to turn to if something adverse happens (data getting lost, laptop stolen, etc.);
- handling requirements for travelling when taking a company laptop or company media;

## 4: General Avoidance and Mitigation Strategies

- detailing what is acceptable use of resources and what is not (such as the private use of e-mail and the Web).

Lastly, please note that introducing additional requirements to a job description may not be easy after the contract has been signed, so it is best to have this ready when the employee signs his/her initial contract.

### A.7.2.1 – Management responsibilities

This control is mainly about requiring employees, contractors and other third parties to apply security as outlined, described (and signed by them) in the various policies and procedures that have been made available to these groups. Strictly speaking, this control is not only to do with requiring these groups to adhere to certain policies and procedures, it is also about supervising and, if necessary, monitoring action carried out. First and foremost, though, you need to require these groups to adhere to your company's policies and procedures as you will otherwise lack the means of following up on an incident or breach.

### A.7.2.2 – Information security awareness, education and training

This control is about training your staff, whether employees, contractors or other third parties, in regard to the information security requirements of your company. Training must be appropriate to the job description, and it is very important to gain agreement on the suitability of training, as nothing is more damaging than people attending irrelevant training, and therefore feeling negative about the whole effort and the goals associated with the effort. The training also needs to be relevant to the job function. For

## 4: General Avoidance and Mitigation Strategies

example, an anti-money-laundering investigating officer will have to receive specialised training (even required by FSA standards), which will be very different from standard training. Networking staff and server operations staff may receive different training, although some common elements will certainly remain (such as explaining the acceptable use policy).

Training must be updated regularly, at least once a year. If you keep your training sessions lively, for instance by including real-life stories and anecdotes, you will find it much easier to raise and maintain an appropriate level of awareness.

### A.7.2.3 – Disciplinary process

There should be a formal disciplinary process in place for a situation where an incident occurs due to severe negligence or even by intent. Making this process transparent is essential in gaining consent and in being able to return to normal once a matter has been dealt with. This transparency is essential if you wish to keep the peace within the enterprise, as it allows everyone to know exactly where they stand.

Please note that, while legislation in some countries is very relaxed on what you can and cannot do regarding a disciplinary process (in the United States, for instance, almost anything can be agreed between the parties), in other countries you will find a strict legal framework limiting your options, such as in Sweden or Germany. In these countries, you will usually have to go to great lengths to be able to fire someone on the spot, requiring a quite

## 4: General Avoidance and Mitigation Strategies

substantial breach of trust (forgetting to lock the computer screen will not suffice).

Let us elaborate on that a little:

- In Sweden, if somebody causes an incident or even a breach due to being drunk, you can fire that person (but not on the spot), even if this only happens once. The moment the employee admits to having a drink problem, however, you cannot fire the person, but have to provide help instead.
- In Germany and Austria, you basically cannot fire a person on the spot. What you can always do, however, is to grant leave of absence starting immediately, and to terminate the contract. Firing on the spot requires a first warning issued to the employee in writing. The warning and its legal effect expire after six months, so only when the same offence is committed within this period, will you be able to declare the employee's contract terminated with immediate effect.
- In the US, you can basically agree on any kind of reason establishing grounds for immediate dismissal, but be aware that, in extreme cases, the affected employee may challenge the legality on ethical grounds (something you can do in any western-style legal system). In the litigation-friendly climate of the US, stipulations regarding immediate dismissal should therefore be precise and checked with a lawyer, to avoid costly lawsuits and even more costly compensation or punitive payments awarded by a court of law.

The core elements of a good disciplinary process are listed below.

## 4: General Avoidance and Mitigation Strategies

- The employee must have the right to be heard and to be assisted by someone of his/her choice.
- A committee, composed of three to five people, depending on the severity of the case, should have the final say.
- All minutes and decisions must be transparent to the employee.
- The employee must have the right to address the committee and make statements.
- The entire process must not be protracted and should be carried out within one month after the incident, the sooner the better.
- The committee must carefully act within the limits of labour law as established in the respective country/jurisdiction.
- The committee must treat the employee with respect. The proceedings are not a court of law, and they must never look or feel like one. If this is not taken into account, severe damage can be caused to company morale and atmosphere.
- All disciplinary punishments must be within the law and appropriate to the incident. A usual 'punishment' for something happening due to negligence, for instance, would simply be retraining.
- The committee must also draft recommendations to the company, if the incident points to a larger problem whose root cause is not the employee's behaviour; for example, if the training the employee had received was found to be flawed or wrong in the first place.

# 4: General Avoidance and Mitigation Strategies

## A.7.3.1 – Termination or change of employment

If an employee's contract is terminated (for whatever reason, whether on friendly or unfriendly terms) it must be clear who is to perform what task in regard to termination. At the end of the day a termination process must:

- be swift and without undue delays
- ensure that assets are returned
- ensure that the employee can provide feedback on their experience (whether terminated on friendly terms or not)
- ensure that access rights are changed properly, if the termination is actually due to a change of position within the corporation, but not a termination in the strict sense.

Responsibilities that need to be defined include those of IT staff, for making the changes required in regard to access rights, and the employee's superior, for collecting items, such as laptops, keys, corporate credit cards and access cards. The employee must also not be able to keep corporate stationery, as this could facilitate all kinds of fraud schemes. IT staff, the superior and a facility management function will usually have roles in a termination or change of employment.

If some requirements (such as confidentiality or a non-competition clause) survive termination of the employment (or freelancing contract) for some time then this should be enforced by, e.g., having the leaving person sign a memorandum reminding him/her of these duties.

As regards changes of employment within the same company, the paramount point to observe is that the change is active by the desired date, so that no productivity is lost. It may well also mean that existing access rights are taken away, if the job description of the employee changes

## 4: General Avoidance and Mitigation Strategies

substantially. For example, if someone moves from the IT department to the Accounts department, it is neither desirable nor necessary for that person to retain administrator access.

### A.8.1.4 – Return of assets

If an employment contract or agreement has been terminated, it must be ensured that all assets are returned on time. These assets include:

- company laptops
- company phones
- company keys and access cards
- company ID card
- company credit cards
- all other items issued to the employee.

It is vital that the company actually knows what has been issued to the employee in the first place. This should be tracked in the employee's personnel file.

In the case of avoiding breaches, if any of the items above has gone missing just before they were due to be returned, you should become very suspicious.

### A.9.2.6 – Removal or adjustment of access rights

It is essential that all access rights are removed promptly if a termination takes place. There are endless stories about former employees still being able to access the network because of forgotten accounts, modems, unchanged firewall rules, and so on.

# 4: General Avoidance and Mitigation Strategies

It is good practice to produce a list of all access rights that have to be removed and work with this as a checklist which, when completed, goes into the personnel file of the employee. In order to be able to do that, however, you need to have documented the access rights at the time they were granted, which is the best method, as documenting access rights after the fact can be very tedious. This is particularly so if NTFS directory and file rights have been used as, once they have been made, there is no efficient way to document them based on a specific user account.

It is also good practice to keep your access rights structure as simple as you can, within the range of what your risk profile allows. There is nothing better than a self-explanatory scheme of access rights. It will simplify, not only removal, but also all kinds of related maintenance tasks, and make them more secure.

**Processes**

This category relates to two major items. Firstly, establishing a security process dealing with the identification of requirements, overseeing their implementation and testing the effectiveness of measures. Secondly, changing established processes to include security elements, such as the four-eyes principle or segregation of duties. A security process will usually take up to two years to become fully operational and effective. Changing existing processes is entirely unpredictable; it could be very quick, if people are already 'on side' or you might have to overcome obstruction from all sides which is usually either due to people not being 'on side' or to political games.

## 4: General Avoidance and Mitigation Strategies

Chapter 6.1 of ISO27001 deals specifically with the details of addressing information security risk. We will skip chapter 6.1.1 as it is too general for inclusion in this book and not topical and will now discuss chapter 6.1.2 – Information security risk assessment in detail:

Please note that ISO 27001:2013 no longer impose a specific risk identification process. It has become more generic as many companies already have some kind of risk identification process in place, be it based on another ISO standard, such as ISO31000, or internal good and best practices; very often it will make total sense to adapt the existing Enterprise Risk Management System to the needs of your ISMS and therefore have a common ground of risk identification instead of two different methodologies. Therefore ISO27001 defines a number of abstract criteria that your risk assessment process must include and that you will find easy to implement, either on their own or by making appropriate links to existing processes for risk identification. These criteria will now be dealt with.

*6.1.2a - Defining risk acceptance criteria and criteria for performing information security risk assessments*

Risk acceptance criteria are those quantitative or qualitative decision making criteria by which you would deem a risk as acceptable or not acceptable. These can be aligned by the expected damage caused by the risk, by strategic evaluation or by purely qualitative criteria. A good starting point is always the question which monetary amount you are

## 4: General Avoidance and Mitigation Strategies

willing to lose should a risk materialize. This will depend on your company's financial strength and its risk appetite.

Criteria for performing information security risk assessments include frequency, risk levels to be used, damage levels to be used, probability levels to be used, staff and functions to be involved, etc.

### 6.1.2b – Ensure comparable results

When you choose your risk assessment methodology you should not only chose qualitative criteria. In information security these make sense very often, but be sure to include some criteria that can be quantified as these offer the benefit of being comparable. Care should be taken anyway, as sometimes, what looks like a sophisticated statistical model is nothing more than blabber or an implementation of the garbage-in garbage-out principle. Chapter 6.1.2b mandates that results from risk assessments product consistent (free from contradictions within themselves), valid and comparable results. This is just the easier to understand as you'd like to know how your ISMS develops, without being able to compare this will not be possible.

### 6.1.2c – Identify risks

Control 6.1.2c mandates that you shall assess risks associated with the loss of confidentiality, integrity and availability of information. This applies primarily to the scope of your ISMS, which opens the possibilities to ignore all risks beyond that scope (especially, if your scope does not cover the entire enterprise), but it would not quite be prudent to do so. It might be less costly, but certainly not

## 4: General Avoidance and Mitigation Strategies

prudent. These risks are also usually associated with specific assets, so you would do your asset identification first, and then assign risk to these assets in the dimensions of confidentiality, integrity, and availability risks.

Control 6.1.2c also requires you to identify risk owners and care should be taken that the roles identified actually makes sense. A risk owner should be a role that actually has power over the risk and can do something about it. It does not make too much sense to identify, e.g. only 'IT Department' as risk owner, this is way too unspecific; something like 'Director IT' or 'System Administrator' will work much better in practice provided that the role has the possibilities and powers to take care of the risk and to remediate it.

So far, we have only identified risks when starting at control 6.1.2a, which is why control 6.1.2d actually requires an analysis of the risks identified in this way:

- assessing the potential consequences, if the risks identified materialized.
- assessing a realistic likelihood of occurrence of the risks.
- determining a level of risk.

In plain English these mean the following. Assessing consequences can be descriptive or quantitative such as cost caused by a risk that has materialized. A descriptive version would be some text describing actual consequence to a business process. In a shortened way one can also define impact categories such as 'legal impact', 'reputational impact', 'purely financial impact', etc.

## 4: General Avoidance and Mitigation Strategies

When determining likelihood of occurrence, one should try to be as precise as possible. It is often a good idea to use fishbone diagrams to find all the circumstances that need to come together to let a particular risk materialize. When doing this you also prevent a not too common, even paranoid, way of thinking which would overestimate risk consequences easily. All security people have an inclination to do that as some results of risk assessments are either counter-intuitive (as in "not as dramatic as one might think") or one would like to use overdramatized risks to ensure appropriate budgets, personnel numbers, etc.

Determining a level of risk refers to making your consideration culminate in such a way that you can classify your risks in levels such as 'irrelevant', 'low', 'medium', 'high', 'existential' or along any other scale that you may feel fit to use or that makes sense in your company or that is mandated by your corporate HQ.

Many times the following way to determine risk levels has been proven as being very practical:

- Firstly, draft a matrix of likelihood vs. impact, if you use 4 levels each your matrix can result in 16 different levels.

- Secondly, the 16 resulting levels you would group depending on how much emphasis you want to put on which risk group. Applying a bit of humour, this is sometimes called the 'paranoia' parameter setting. In practical terms your matrix might have 4 levels ranging from 'low', 'elevated', 'medium', 'high' for each, the likelihood and the impact category, and therefore you would group in such a way that, maybe, only a high/high combination counts as highest relevance level or that anything from

## 4: General Avoidance and Mitigation Strategies

'medium' to 'high' for each category constitutes the highest relevance level.

- Thirdly, you would then group your risks in a new matrix with your relevance level as one axis and mitigation cost as a second axis. From this matrix you would be able to see which risks can be remediated in an affordable way and which can't; thereby you would directly arrive at a business priority decision since any risk of high relevance but with a low mitigation cost should be handled first whereas risks whose mitigation cost is too high can't be handled (they must be accepted) and risks for which the relevance factor is low do not need to be handled.

What 6.1.2d refers to is actually the outcome of the second step. Once you've done this you have actually sorted your risks by relevance and assigned a risk level.

What we called step 3 above is actually contained in control 6.1.2e which mandates evaluation of information security risks based on the criteria you have established in 6.1.2a and with the priorities you arrived at through step 3. The control just states that you should prioritize the analysed risks for treatment, which is exactly what you arrive at applying the third step above.

### Chapter 6.1.3 – Risk Treatment

ISO27001 requires you to apply a risk treatment process to deal with the risks that you have analysed applying control 6.1.2. This process does not need to be a process of its own

## 4: General Avoidance and Mitigation Strategies

in your process landscape, the steps required can be embedded in other operational process or in an existing enterprise risk treatment process. What this control wants that process to achieve is the following:

- Selecting appropriate options based on your assessment results. Such options can include technical means, physical means, easy means such as re-training because lack of training was found to be a risk factor for a particular risk, etc.

- Determining all controls that are necessary to implement to appropriately treat the risks identified. This requires a bit more explanation as the Standard does not only provide a set of controls, it does require your organisation to think, if any new or modified controls need to be applied to your specific risk situation, which are not yet contained in the Standard. If you come across such a control the expectation is that you define and implement it. You can choose controls from any source you see fit.

- Comparing the controls you have identified with Annex A of the Standard to ensure that you have not omitted any that might be necessary. So, you might have additional controls, but you should not have fewer controls than Annex A contains unless you can prove that one or more controls are not applicable to your risk situation.

- Production of a statement of applicability that contains all controls chosen and a justification for their inclusion. This statement must also contain information on whether the control is implemented

## 4: General Avoidance and Mitigation Strategies

or not and justifications for any exclusions you may have made, e.g., as an ISP without your own software development department you will de-select all control pertaining to software development security. When providing information on a control's implementation status you can use a scale such as 'implemented', 'in progress', 'not implemented'. Generally, it is not advisable to lie about implementation status or to exaggerate it. At the latest in the Stage-2 audit your auditors will find out, and is usually better to assure auditor goodwill by being fully, or at least reasonably, open about your actual state of implementation.

This statement of applicability is a formal requirement for certification and together with your information security policy, your risk assessment and risk treatment plan the most important document of your ISMS.

- Formulation of an information security risk treatment plan.

This plan is the central summary about how you intend to remediate the risks identified. It will usually contain the risk, the control, the role responsible for implementation, a timeline by which remediation should have taken place and a reference to an internal project or task implementing the control.

- Obtaining risk owner approval.

Once the risk treatment plan is set up and the residual risks have been worked out including those that need to be or can be accepted, the risk owner

## 4: General Avoidance and Mitigation Strategies

will approve of the risk treatment plan and formally sign off on risk acceptance for those risks for which acceptance is the most appropriate way of dealing with.

It should be mentioned that you need to retain documented information about your risk treatment process, it will be closely examined in your company's Stage-1 audit and without proper documentation you will find it hard or impossible to arrive at comparable results and to be able to demonstrate a working ISMS. On a very personal level, as a CISO, ISO, or CSO this may even influence your bonus regulations.

Generally, you will usually update your risk profile about once a year, but we will recommend, as rule, that you update twice a year or whenever an incident has shown that your risk mitigation process (the implementation of the risk treatment plan) did not live up to its originally designed level.

In closing, here are some examples of triggers which will cause you to update parts or all of your risk profile:

- setting up a new site; particularly if that site is in a dangerous country.
- adding new technology to your infrastructure, such as WLAN or Java-enabled smartphones.
- changes to the departmental structure of the company.
- changes to procedural practices in the company, e.g. the introduction of teleworking.
- special circumstances, such as hiring a large number of employees at one time, or downsizing substantially.
- changes to the regulatory framework of your business.

## 4: General Avoidance and Mitigation Strategies

**Technology**

The minimum requirements for a medium- to large-sized company today can be expressed by listing the following technologies which should be present:

- firewalls implementing zoning according to security classifications
- intrusion prevention
- switched networks
- virus protection for file systems, e-mail and http(s) traffic
- spam filtering
- log file consolidation
- system monitoring
- single sign-on
- data leakage prevention

Admittedly, data leakage prevention is a very new field, but it has achieved stunning success at very reasonable cost. Today, it is actually possible to have software installed that will recognise classified documents and prevent – among other things – copy-and-paste from such documents.

While the first three elements will ensure that your network remains secure, the following take care of your server and client systems, with data leakage prevention products bridging the gap with the human being.

### *ISO27001 Controls helpful for treatment of breaches*

Of the 114 controls in ISO27001:2013, 15 deal with aspects that relate to the treatment of information security breaches. ISO 27001:2013, as a great step forward from the 2005 version, has included an entire chapter on information

## 4: General Avoidance and Mitigation Strategies

security incident management, which will be the focal point of this chapter of this book. But first, those controls of the Standard that are helpful individually and play a big role in coping with a breach.

### A.6.1.3 – Contact with authorities

ISO27001 stipulates that your company should maintain ties with relevant authorities. This is not always possible, and in some countries it is even illegal. You should therefore maintain close ties where you can, and try to be as knowledgeable as possible about the general investigative processes employed by the authorities. This will help you conduct an investigation swiftly and without friction. Do not underestimate the effect of keeping informal ties, sometimes simply called 'knowing someone'. While you should never try to get favours from your contacts (as this might make you guilty of a criminal offence), understanding each other's way of thinking speeds up the flow of action considerably. In additional, the modus operandi of criminals who have been caught is usually shared between police and companies, and businesses can gain a considerable benefit from understanding how criminal elements try to subvert their services.

### A.7.2.2 – Information security awareness, education and training

Making sure that you have an appropriate IS awareness programme is quite likely to prevent incidents, and is essential to ensure proper reaction to breaches. A good programme achieves the following:

## 4: General Avoidance and Mitigation Strategies

- short reaction times for reporting incidents to the right people through the right channels; 'right' in the sense of 'defined'.
- a general sense of what to do when an incident occurs.
- clear directions in regard to disciplinary processes for those committing breaches that can lead, or have led, to incidents.

### A.7.2.3 – Disciplinary process
### A.8.1.4 – Return of assets
### A.9.2.6 – Removal or adjustment of access rights

These controls were discussed earlier in this chapter.

### A.12.2.1 – Controls against malware

It must be ensured that the environment is free from viruses, Trojans, Worms and APTs, as these are a prime means of extracting data from a company. Active measures must also be taken against root kits. If a company has lost data through theft, and viruses cannot be ruled out as a means of operation, the investigation will become infinitely difficult, as it has to check for this potential cause of information leaks. If the source cannot be narrowed down to a team or department then, in the worst case, you might find yourself having to examine all the computers in your company for the existence of viruses or Trojans.

You should also ensure that you have a defined recovery process in place to cleanse your systems of viruses, root kits, and so on, in the case of a successful virus attack. In practice, this may mean having disk images or other means of restoration ready for redeployment on client or server

## 4: General Avoidance and Mitigation Strategies

machines. This control also emphasises the need for good system documentation, so that you can recover speedily.

### A.12.4.1 – Event logging and
### A-12.4.3 – Administrator and operator logs

Having log files is an essential proactive means of security and incident resolution. Without logging there is simply no available means for investigators to delve into events of the past. The quality of what is logged determines its worth for an investigation; the more, the better, limited only by applicable data protection laws.

We also mention keeping administrator and operator logs here because you, the company, must have a chance to differentiate actions performed by potential intruders from regular, normal, activities. If not, your analysis will be full of false positives, which basically brings the value of the analysis to down to nil.

### A.12.4.2 – Protection of log information

A log file's worth can be greatly decreased and even voided if it has been tampered with or damaged. It is important to keep log files safe and secure by applying MD5 hashing or by using other means, such as writing them on one-time-write media, such as CDs or DVDs, to ensure that they cannot be tampered with once written. A smart perpetrator might try to lay false trails by tampering with log files. Today it is best practice to use software that will safeguard your log files by hashing automatically.

The following controls are those directly relevant to the treatment of information security breaches and are based on

## 4: General Avoidance and Mitigation Strategies

Chapter 16 of the Standard – Information security incident management. On a lighter note, this chapter having been included as a chapter of its own in the 2013 version of ISO27001 indicates that there was a certain need to have it. In other words, as long as new breaches are reported on more or less every week, this chapter has all the right in the world to exist.

### *A.16.1.1 – Responsibilities and procedures*

The Standard recommends that responsibilities and procedures for incident handling be clearly defined and in such a way that a quick, effective, and orderly response can be assured. While it may sound trivial at first, the level of nervousness or sheer panic that can arise during a breach is a problem in itself and hence having all these responsibilities and processes clearly defined is a major step in reducing mistakes during the incident/breach and ensuring that no one will lose his or her head during the breach. Just recently, during the Heartbleed global disaster it became apparent once more how much better properly prepared companies can deal with such an incident compared to those who aren't (thereby minimising their incident costs).

Let's take a deeper look at what 'quick', 'effective'" and 'orderly' are supposed to mean, starting with 'orderly' as it is the easiest to define. In plain English, it means having a process in place that is good enough, so that people are able to and will follow it. 'Orderly' also implies that people have received training on the process and that you, as manager, have sufficient assurance that the process, once needed, can and will be carried out swiftly, without panic, and without major surprises. Minor surprises will occur because

## 4: General Avoidance and Mitigation Strategies

breaches are not really predictable (depending on the type of breach: some are a bit predictable), but major surprises which drive the company into a panic or bring it to a standstill must not occur.

'Quick' refers to the fact that it should not take a long time for anything to happen. The reporting line should be short and driven by competent people -for as long as the breach exists; a shortened version of the standard reporting line could even be used to make sure no time is lost . 'Quick' also means that an executive should make a fast decision on who is on the breach handling team and for practical purposes this group should not exceed eight people; if more people have to be involved, it is better for form sub-groups than to have one huge group of 20 or more people who – in today's interconnected world – might find it hard to coordinate.

'Effective' refers to ensuring, by means of planning and carrying out exercises, that the procedures in place actually do contribute to better the situation and not to making it worse. This **will** happen in companies that either do not have the procedures required, have never tried them or have neglected training.

One last thing of quite some importance: make sure that these roles and responsibilities are reviewed once in a while (typically yearly) or every time significant changes to the infrastructure or process landscape are made. A change must at least be deemed significant if, due to the change, roles, responsibilities or procedures that exist need to be fundamentally changed to adapt to it.

*4: General Avoidance and Mitigation Strategies*

### A.16.1.2 – Reporting information security events

This is quite a standard operating control, stipulating that a process should exist to report security events, independent of their nature. While most events will be treated through standard operational channels, for instance, the team responsible for server or network operations, a substantial breach may first be noticed because of a comparatively minor event at a lower level. This control includes the reporting requirement for severe breaches and incidents. You should therefore ensure that a clear reporting process exists and that the parameters for categorising events are clear and are understood by all affected.

### A.16.1.3 – Reporting security weaknesses

A weakness, as opposed to an event, is a condition a system is found to be in, for example, due to a lack of updates applied or a lack of patches. While referring primarily to technical weaknesses, you should go so far as to consider the absence of an application of the four-eyes principle as a weakness, too. Organisational weaknesses exist, just as much as technical weaknesses, and that is exactly how they should be viewed and named, to ensure that they receive sufficient management attention.

### A.16.1.4 – Assessment of and decision on information security events

The Standard uses an implicit order of things, namely an 'event' is something less than an 'incident'. What we call 'breach' in this book, the Standard would call ''incident', but as you can see from the case studies, we consider a breach to be a special type of incident, namely one in which

## 4: General Avoidance and Mitigation Strategies

potential consequences are very severe from the very outset.

Now, since in practice many companies have implemented logging systems but neither the technology nor the staffing to actually evaluate and monitor these logging systems, the 2013 version of ISO27001 makes it clear that you must make an informed decision on whether an event that has been identified needs to be treated as an incident (or even breach). Do not underestimate this. This is an intellectually challenging task that requires human guidance and judgement. For example, one minor event may still be treated as a minor event whereas thousands of minor events at the same time either indicate a fault in configuring the logging systems (causing negligible events to be recorded as something greater than they are, for instance) or that an incident is unfolding. Also, declaring something an incident will require a business decision based on the infrastructure or application affected. There might be good reasons not to (immediately) shut down a particular application or infrastructure event though an incident is unfolding.

### *A.16.1.5 – Response to information security incidents*

This control is a bit trivial, as it just states that responding to an incident should follow documented procedures. As trivial as it may sound, it still contains two layers of truth:

1.) Following established procedures is a safeguard against individual and corporate liability. If you can show that you followed the procedures in place you have nothing to fear as an individual or a company (as long as these procedures are at least somewhat plausible and correct). It is quite typical for breach

## 4: General Avoidance and Mitigation Strategies

management procedures to allow the actual **lifting** of procedures during a breach when this is the only path forward to resolution. If such a decision is made, it will be made by the Incident Management Board / Information Security Incident Management Board or sometimes even the Business Continuity Board depending on the severity of the breach; under no circumstances should an individual feel entitled not to stick to a given procedure, if only for his/her own protection.

2.) The control implies that such procedures exist. This might be a challenge for some companies, but common sense and the situation laid out in point 1 should make it pretty clear that there is no leeway about this.

### *A.16.1.6 – Learning from information security incidents*

Once an incident (or breach) has been contained or resolved, it is vital that those lessons which can be learned from it really are learned. Only in rare cases are there no lessons to be learned, and this is the exception, not the rule. The company also needs to ensure that it can implement whatever requirements form the outcome of this learning phase, whether additional training, new systems, or perhaps changes to existing systems or processes.

### *A.16.1.7 – Collection of evidence*

ISO27001 stipulates that the company needs to know the rules which apply to the collection of evidence in the jurisdictions that it operates in. It is absolutely necessary to

## 4: General Avoidance and Mitigation Strategies

undertake this task. Not all companies may wish to take their breaches to court, but, once you do, you need to be certain that the evidence collected throughout the investigation is admissible in court. If it turns out not to be, the court will turn in another direction – against you.

It should be noted that international companies will have to first establish the number of jurisdictions they are exposed to, and get proper legal support for all of these. Smaller companies might find it hard to gain full support at reasonable prices and, in this regard, these companies usually take higher risks. For the purposes of investigating breaches, at least being aware of such issues is half the bill paid.

### Strategies and tactics for treating breaches

There are a number of main strategies and tactics to apply after a breach has occurred.

#### Get the 6 Ws immediately

Not *as soon as possible*, as this would include *never*, but *immediately*. These 6 Ws are:

- What has happened? Get full details in as little time as possible, but allow enough time to get the truth. A first description, given in panic, can lead the subsequent efforts of mitigation in a false direction.
- Who/What is affected? Who could be the perpetrator?
- When did it happen? This can be tricky, as some breaches, such as break-ins, might be well hidden, however, you need to establish the time line correctly.
- Where did it happen? Which locations are affected?
- Why did it happen? This summarises technical root causes, as well as intentional or accidental human

## 4: General Avoidance and Mitigation Strategies

actions. Once answered, you will have a clearer picture on future avoidance, and you may get important input to catch the perpetrator.
- How much? Primarily, this refers to damage. What damage is to be expected or what has already occurred? Secondarily, it also refers to the emergency budget you may need to cope with the situation. As a rule of thumb you can count on the following:
  - Damage increases exponentially, if an entire business process is affected. After three days, it can already be threatening the very existence of your company.
  - Just like in a wildfire, you might have to 'cut' network connections or 'dig a trench' by isolating unaffected networks to keep the damage from spreading, for instance, when a very new, sophisticated virus hits.
  - Emergency budgets for investigations are usually in the five-figure range. For very complex cases either requiring a lot of information gathering through non-conventional channels, or involving international travel at short notice, or a requirement for a lot of technical equipment, a case budget can easily reach the lower six figures (with a limit of about £300,000). Extensive investigations involving corporate fraud, including all the roles, people and time needed, can be said to be limited around £10 million. Subsequent legal fees will easily exceed that figure. Our explanations on emergency budgets do not include the cost of re-establishing infrastructure or company services. It would be wise to reserve up to 10% of your IT budget for that on a yearly basis. You can still save it or spend it on more urgent items should no incidents occur. Be advised, however, that your

## 4: General Avoidance and Mitigation Strategies

infrastructure might have details so intricate and arcane that 10% might not suffice, due to a lack of documentation.

**Establish a team** (a task force) to cope with the breach.

Do not let an individual make emergency decisions; they may be overwhelmed by the sudden burden of responsibility. At least, that is the most likely response of an employee who is untrained in emergency situations. Install a team of senior management and relevant internal experts to cope with the situation. You may wish to add a steering committee for genuinely sensitive discussions, such as whether the incident/breach happened due to internal factors.

**Resolution first – blame later** (or never)

Trying to get a handle on the breach should be your first priority. Ultimately, as time and the investigation into the breach will show, there will be consequences for someone; perhaps soft ones, such as retraining, but maybe even firings, or criminal and civil proceedings against external or internal people. Try to abstain from blaming anyone before all facts are known, however, as you will only ruin what is left of the company climate.

In fact, try to abstain from blame altogether, if possible, and focus on the lessons to be learned and on implementing them correctly. This excludes criminal acts, of course, but we are focusing here on distributing – or rather not distributing – internal blame.

**Establish lessons learned**

As we are dealing with breaches, it may well be the case that there are no more lessons to be learned, as the company goes bankrupt. Some breaches (*see the case studies in Part 2*), however, do leave room for survival which is, of course, a good thing. So, from quite early on in the process of recovering from an incident, try to establish what needs to be learned to stop the same, or a similar, incident from recurring.

**Get PR involved**

If you have a PR department, get them involved quite early in the process of recovering from, or investigating, a breach, so that they can prepare for interviews, public statements of senior management or even responses to unfavourable media reports. As a company, you should be ahead of events not driven by them, and you need to communicate clearly and unambiguously about your situation, if need be, to keep to a minimum damage to your customers' trust and that of the public.

**Be prepared**

The best choice of all is to have a well-trained security team in place, and to run paper-based or real-life emergency exercises from time to time. These exercises should focus on potential breach scenarios, not standard ones. For additional precision, study the results with external professionals, to add an unbiased view of the scenario and its results. Preparedness also applies to all other employees, and the minimum level would be for everyone to know whom to call and what to report.

# 4: General Avoidance and Mitigation Strategies

**Tactical advice**

*Regular meetings*

Have the investigational team meet every day, maybe even twice a day (in the morning and in the evening) to elaborate on expectations and the results of the day, share information, align along a common view and decide on the priorities of the next days or weeks. There will be phases when such daily meetings are absolutely necessary.

*Time, time, time*

All information must be reported in a timely manner, and all steps of the investigation must be carried out in time. When a breach has occurred there is no time to waste, as the perpetrator has already shown that they have an advantage over the victim, simply by accomplishing the breach. Time, or time lost, will add to that advantage.

*Rest*

It is just a myth that any human being can work for longer than 24 hours and expect their work results to remain good. Investigations are entirely unforgiving when it comes to mistakes (give away your cover when performing surveillance and, as a result, the surveillance operation, or even the case, may be blown). This means that you need to make sure your people are at the top of their game. The team should be properly staffed in terms of numbers, and people should be allowed to rest. Experience has shown that it might even be a good idea to employ the submariner's four- or eight-hour shifts, as better adapted to standard office life. A four-hour shift would mean four hours of work followed by four hours of rest. This would mean that during a 24-hour period, an investigator would have two or three four-hour working shifts.

*People (number)*

Make sure enough people are assigned to the case; make sure they can contribute, and make sure they can work as a team. In the emergency that a breach creates, the people may not yet have defined themselves as a team, but there is not actually much room to do so. In that case, appoint a clearly-defined leader with appropriate powers.

*International contacts*

Many breaches and cyber crime scenarios involve international gangs or people operating from a foreign country. Make sure that you can establish, or that you already have, good international contacts, either through investigational agencies or through your staff or external lawyers. This will greatly improve your ability to follow up internationally on the breach and to guide other countries' police forces through the case. Remember that, in some countries, police forces may still not be sufficiently trained to deal with these new types of crime and corruption.

*Keep the information flowing*

All those relevant to resolving the breach should have the same level of information, or at least a level of information that enables them to actively support all efforts at resolution. The situation becomes more difficult when

## 4: General Avoidance and Mitigation Strategies

internals might be involved in causing the breach, since you will then have to compartmentalise information, but this should be a last resort.

Within the investigational team, information should flow freely at any given time, so that everybody can get themselves up to speed if, for example, they may have missed a meeting for operational reasons.

*Keep minutes*

Make sure that deliberations and decisions of the investigational team or task force are recorded, by assigning the role of minute-keeper to someone. This person should then do nothing but keep the minutes, in order not to be distracted by another role and its duties. If minutes cannot be kept in writing, try recording sound or (preferably) video. The purpose is quality assurance of the investigation and to know, verbatim, what has been decided and why.

*Additional quality feedback*

It makes sense to have one experienced extra investigator on the team to provide feedback on decisions and deliberations. While not being directly involved, this person can provide valuable input, and will be essential in keeping the investigation fault free, especially when tempers are fraught, or if people are not yet sufficiently experienced in handling investigations. This extra person might see something the team has overlooked, and could provide feedback on the overall quality of the investigation based on an experience level of 15 to 20 years. Having quality feedback as the investigation proceeds ensures that subsequent steps have a higher success rate. This person

## 4: General Avoidance and Mitigation Strategies

should be consulted before all decisions which would result in a major shift of focus or line of action in the investigation.

## Dimensions of treatment / mitigation of information security breaches

When dealing with incidents and breaches the following dimensions of treatment exist:

- none
- internal investigation
- external investigation
- joint task force.

### *None*

To be frank, it can sometimes happen that there are no options for treatment, or that the investigation has to stop at a certain point, for lack of further facts or for company political reasons. It is, however, rare that absolutely nothing can be done about an incident or about preventing it from recurring. Thinking hard about root causes can already bring success in that small area, but it is possible that you will run out of options quite early in the investigation. For instance, the perpetrator could hide in a foreign country where there is weak legislation, or the company needs to be relocated because of a flood, but that is not possible. In such a case it is still important to have all deliberations documented, so that it can be explained to an external tax auditor or a court of law why an investigative operation was stopped, or why no further measures were put in place.

# 4: General Avoidance and Mitigation Strategies

## Internal investigation

An internal investigation should be set up as a team effort, staffed as described below.

- A leader, who should be knowledgeable in investigational techniques and capable of guiding people. This person should possess strong social skills, to keep the investigation on track.
- Depending on the size of the incident, someone to track activities, and produce and keep records to enable lessons to be learned.
- A number of technical experts as required by the nature of the incident. In larger incidents, the following is a good starting point:
  - an expert in networks and network protocols;
  - an operating systems expert (maybe even one per operating system involved, e.g. Microsoft® Windows® Server 2003, Red Hat Linux);
  - an application level expert, if applications are involved. For instance, someone who knows about the inner workings of the SAP implementation in the specific environment.

A typical team would consist of three people for small incidents, and up to a dozen members for larger cases.

It should be decided, early on in the process, whether the incident will end up in court, as courts of law have their own rules in regard to the preservation, evaluation and admissibility of evidence, among many other aspects. Once this has been established, additional experienced personnel should be included for continuous quality feedback on the investigation, and for review to ensure that the decisions made are always as correct as possible. Breaches are not forgiving when it comes to mistakes made in the investigation. Small mistakes have the potential to invalidate an entire investigation later on, or to lead the action off in the wrong direction.

## *External investigation*

Some cases should not be handled internally, owing to the sensitivity of the subject. In general, every severe breach involving an employee should be handled under the leadership of external investigators, as they tend to be quicker to uncover the truth. The team needs to be supported by internals in terms of getting to know the organisational structure and technical aspects of affected systems, but must enact all measures independently and under the approval of senior management. External investigators should also be called in if a matter is too politically sensitive for internals to deal with, or if the company just does not have the necessary know-how.

## *Joint task force*

A joint task force of internals and externals will only be required if the incident threatens the existence of the company, or if the company simply cannot provide the necessary expertise through internal resources alone. A typical joint task force would include:

- the investigating team
- a market communications expert or team
- the head of the department affected
- the CSO or CISO or another senior manager
- the CFO for ad hoc financial decisions

## 4: General Avoidance and Mitigation Strategies

Regardless of chosen methods, the investigating team needs to accomplish the goals below.

- Find the root cause of the incident.
- Track down the root cause, for instance, to a person, a technical system or a process weakness. There should be agreement in the team about this root cause; any differences of opinion should be noted in the documentation.
- In cases involving criminal actions: gather and follow up on the evidence as much as allowed by the investigations budget, which should be set up in advance and should provide reasonable resources. The minimum budget is usually £40–60,000 for larger cases, and can easily climb to six figures.
- Clearly document constraints on the investigation itself.

# PART 2 – CASE STUDIES

## CHAPTER 5: NOTES FROM THE FIELD

This chapter will present some of the substantial differences that exist between a police investigation and a private one, as one or the other usually follows a breach. It seems necessary to point out these differences, to provide the reader with a better understanding of the available options.

### Privacy

Strange as it may sound, you should carefully weigh the risk of your situation getting more publicity than you wish for, if you report it to the authorities. If your case is high profile enough, either due to the nature of the breach (such as 100 million credit card records stolen) or due to the fact that your company is well known (a Fortune 500 company or the national equivalent), the likelihood of it becoming public is almost 100 per cent, due to the large base of people affected and the tendency of the press to have sources almost everywhere. If your case is of a smaller scale or not overly complex, then the benefit of a private investigation, which usually has much stricter non-disclosure rules and reports to you only, should be carefully weighed against the benefit or impact of reporting it to the authorities. Under no circumstances should you fail to report your case if you have a regulatory duty to do so.

# 5: Notes from the Field

## Cost

Let us be honest, a police investigation has one big advantage. It will not cost you a penny apart from the work needed to provide evidence from records that you would have had to produce anyway, whichever way you decided to investigate the matter. If you are really cost-sensitive and if there are no other disadvantages in reporting a case to the police, you should do so.

## The practicalities of surveillance

In many cases, it will become necessary to carry out fairly long-term surveillance operations on subjects. This may mean over an extended period of time, or just at some critical points in time as events unfold. There are substantial differences between surveillance operations carried out by police and those carried out by private investigators, as is described below.

### *People*

A police observation team will consist of 10 to 15 people per subject. They will employ several vehicles and work 24-hour shifts if needed.

A private observation team consists of no more than two people and will employ no more than two vehicles at any given moment. Usually, though, teams will be changed so as not to arouse suspicion. A private investigation team will hardly ever work 24-hour shifts, and will usually perform observation between 6 a.m. and 10 p.m., so the usual observation period is 16 hours.

# 5: Notes from the Field

## Cost

While a police surveillance operation comes at no cost at all for you, a private observation will cost around £3,000 per day, per subject. The cost can be higher if international travel is involved. This cost is largely due to the fact that two people are needed for the observation period, and this is also the reason why an observation team is based on two people.

## Speed

On this point, the private sector is clearly the winner. The private investigation team will care about you only, as you are the customer. You will be high priority, and everything you need will be carried out promptly and without much ado. That, unfortunately, cannot be said for a police investigation, where their assessment of the priority of your case may be quite different from your own.

## Outreach

Again, the private sector has an advantage here. Good investigation companies have a very tight national and international network of information sources that can speedily and accurately provide much needed information during an investigation. Do not forget, though, that information in a private investigation always comes at a cost; it is not free, nor can anybody be forced to give out information.

# 5: Notes from the Field

## The truth vs. company policy

While the police are sworn to do their best to follow up on crime, and it is even a basic element of the judicial process (for crimes) to get to the truth of the matter, that may not be what you want as a company. Sometimes, you may only wish the damage to be contained, or you may just wish to get enough details to base further decisions on. In short, using a private investigation company you will always be on top of the investigation and be able to steer it. This is what you lose when you turn to the police, as all control is taken out of your hands. This can have some basic side-effects with regard to publicity, and on the case as a whole. If you want to remain in charge, employ private investigators for as long as you can.

Depending on jurisdiction, reporting requirements for suspected crimes involving theft of customer information may and do exist. As a company, you might be required to report the suspected crime to the authorities and you may have to inform affected customers.

# CHAPTER 6: MOTIVES AND REASONS

Breaches do not just happen. Breaches are committed. They are committed by determined people and facilitated by a lack of measures in one of the areas introduced in Part 1 (people, processes and technology). In this chapter, we will be taking a detailed look into the motives of people who have committed breaches, and into the basic reasons why they were able to succeed. An in-depth analysis of the author's archives has shown that all motives can be narrowed down to four basic ones, all of them very, very human: greed, despair, a disgruntled employee seeking revenge and too lazy to remain honest, or the desire to gain an unjust business advantage. Let's look at these in more detail.

## Greed

A very basic human motive, this, and basically the other side of a coin called ambition. Information security breaches involving greed include cases about information sold for pure profit (such as the banking information sold to secret services and tax authorities in 2009 and 2010, or a sales manager changing companies and selling information to his new employer in the process); and cases where the main motive was purely financial with no other motive in place. These cases are usually facilitated by a missing access rights regime, a lack of access rights or by people having excessive access rights (more than they need to perform their job function).

# 6: Motives and Reasons

The greed scenario also applies to cases of corporate corruption, kick-back schemes, and so on.

## Despair

From time to time it happens that someone has far too ambitious plans for their own life (usually regarding material wealth), then finds themselves entangled in a web of debt without a hope of escape. In such a situation, people become vulnerable to the attraction of taking a short cut, and sell company information for their own profit to get out of their debt situation. The vulnerability is usually limited to those who are weak of character, as other people may not have got themselves into such trouble in the first place, or would be strong enough to seek help. Other related motives include gambling addictions and other situations where people spend more money than they can afford (including alcohol and drug addictions). In the case studies, we have included one such case, where financial problems made an employee sell out information to the competition.

As for facilitating factors: these are the same as in the greed scenario. The employee usually has too much access to information (especially valuable material) without proper limits having been set.

## Revenge

In companies without a positive, people focused culture, employees can become disgruntled from time to time. For some companies this can be seen as inherent in the business model as, for example, in call centres whose working conditions are often less than ideal, whereas other

## 6: Motives and Reasons

companies may suddenly be hit by the actions of a disgruntled employee, and not have seen it coming.

The underlying scenarios of a disgruntled-employee situation include:

- employees who have been passed over for promotion;
- long-serving employees who have a new boss with whom they do not get on;
- employees who feel they have been wronged in some way, perhaps to do with career, pay raises, or purely social items, such as another employee getting a parking space while not having one themselves;
- employees who know they will be laid off without good explanation;
- employees who do not feel appreciated for their work over a long period of time.

Disgruntled employees can 'strike back' at the company in one of several ways. They may try to sell information, but they are usually more determined to cause damage to satisfy their need for revenge. This damage could be something to bring down services or servers, bring viruses into the network, or it may involve actions which have nothing to do with IT, such as contacting the media over some company dirty laundry, or helping the competition by selling or providing company information.

Breaches committed by disgruntled employees are facilitated by a general lack of information security management controls. They are hard to predict, as the employee may either go for destructive action or action discussed under the earlier 'Greed' paragraph. In any case, the employee will exceed their permissions and use every possible loophole in the controls to get the desired revenge.

## 6: Motives and Reasons

Unfortunately, even looking through my pile of case statistics, the picture does not get much clearer. About half of cases involving disgruntled employees related to stolen data, while the other half were about bringing down the IT infrastructure of the company in some way.

As part of a risk analysis, it may even be worthwhile putting yourself in the position of a disgruntled employee, and using the job descriptions available to look into what such an employee could actually do. This would help you in refining controls to protect against disgruntled employees, whose behaviour is extremely unpredictable; even the most introverted employee may be pushed over the edge by some internal company development.

**Business advantage**

Today, industrial espionage has been made easier by the possibilities offered by information technology. This should be a real concern for companies, and not only the large ones; consider all the former intelligence agents now out of work and looking for job opportunities elsewhere. The previous decade (2000 to 2009) saw a dramatic increase in industrial espionage facilitated by these former agents. It should be noted, however, that western countries also support 'business intelligence'. This whole field started in the US, with companies setting up entire departments to get ahead of the competition by finding out what they were up to. These business intelligence departments usually rely on the following means:

- Social engineering methods, ranging from making official visits to plants and asking questions of unwary

## 6: Motives and Reasons

tour guides, up to infiltrating a company with spying employees.
- Public sources, such as the Web and a company's home page, but also social media pages of people known to be employees.
- Intelligence sources, such as eavesdropping and spying on mail.
- Bribery or other completely illegal methods.

The past years since the first edition of this book have seen a continued increase in demand for anti-eavesdropping equipment and services. This is not surprising, as companies of all sizes are being spied on, provided they are deemed a lucrative target. Furthermore, a whole industry of information brokering has developed with rather dubious figures offering company information on web forum based black markets.

The underlying motive for industrial espionage is always the same: while developing a product may cost millions or even billions, stealing its specifications from the competition is much cheaper, and infinitely more cost effective. While it may be possible to root out all the other scenarios mentioned so far by having special programmes in place addressing people's needs at the workplace, gaining a business advantage by spying is such a fundamental act that it will always be necessary to have a good information security management system in place.

Technically speaking, industrial espionage is facilitated by the following factors:
- a lack of physical security;
- a lack of screening of new personnel, particularly temporary staff;

## 6: Motives and Reasons

- a lack of awareness concerning social engineering;
- a lack of limitation of access rights;
- a lack of monitoring systems to detect breaches on a timely basis;
- a lack of a humane culture, with a number of staff members bearing grudges against the company for whatever reason.

# CHAPTER 7: CASE STUDIES FROM SMALL COMPANIES

**Foreword to the case studies**

The following chapters present case studies of information security breaches from all sectors of the economy, arranged by the size of the company affected.

Names and places have been changed to protect the identity of the victims.

The stories have been slightly dramatised to make them more readable, but all essential facts have remained unaltered, and took place as described.

The case studies contain a description of the events, followed by an in-depth explanation, and a separate section on lessons learned, where applicable.

**The stolen backup**

All was well at Peter B's computer repair shop, in this city of 2 million inhabitants, somewhere in Europe. His shop specialised in computer equipment used mainly by the printing sector, and he had excellent relations with all the relevant newspapers and publishing houses. In fact, his company's success was mainly based on his reputation within this sector of the economy.

But Peter B's business was limited by the size of this sector, and the shop, while successful, did not have much opportunity for substantial growth. He was never going to be able to employ more than three people, and business

## 7: Case Studies from Small Companies

revenue was about 3 million euros in good years, and about 1 million euros in those years when repair budgets were cut, or when his clients' equipment failed less often.

It is important to note that Peter B was a bit hot-headed and his employees could feel that from time to time. He was very often a little short tempered and, as this was his shop and his alone, he could be somewhat dictatorial in his decision making. To anyone who knew all of the people involved, the following events were fairly predictable.

One summer's morning, Peter B came into his shop to find the following:

- none of the three computers used for administering the shop would boot up;
- all customer and accounting records (paper) were gone;
- his long-term employee, Alex D, did not show up for work and did not respond to telephone calls.

It was immediately clear that the month-long quarrels between Peter B and Alex D had turned very sour.

At this point, there was not much to be done, beyond getting the computers to work again. Without bothering too much about correct forensic procedures, the computers were reinstalled and some data recovery attempted, but that mostly failed, due to the prior reinstallation of the operating system. Some data could, however, be restored, but to restore the database of contacts (which was easier) and the database of outstanding repair orders and conditions (which was the hard part), Peter B mostly had to rely on customers coming in, or customers calling to complain about missed meetings and delivery deadlines for equipment repairs.

Things turned even sourer as it became clear that Alex D was about to open his own shop, using the stolen customer

## 7: Case Studies from Small Companies

information to lure customers away by offering them prices at around 30% of the rate that Peter B charged.

That plan failed as, in this case, customers showed considerable loyalty once they had the full picture of what had happened. Such customer loyalty is exceptional, and cannot be included as a mitigating factor in a risk analysis because of its inherent unreliability. Alex D's repair shop went bankrupt after six months, following heavy price competition between the two shop owners.

In total, it took about three months to fully restore operations at Peter B's shop, largely due the combined lack of computer and paper information, and because an external backup (such as storing tapes in his own home) simply did not exist.

### *In-depth explanation*

The damage in this case was multiple and illustrates, on a comparatively small scale, the extent of such incidents.

- Where available, customer data had to be restored from delivery receipts, invoices, or simply by waiting for customers to complain that their repairs had not been finished on time; a tedious, manual process.
- Many customers needed to be contacted personally to re-establish basic facts, such as addresses, telephone numbers, and bank account data.
- The tax authorities had to be spoken to, to explain delays in VAT transfers which, in City X, are due monthly.
- Customers had to be convinced that normal operations would resume soon. Fear of potential loss of trust is an aggravating factor at this point in such cases.

## 7: Case Studies from Small Companies

- Peter B did, in fact, lose some customers. Alex D's pricing presented Peter B with the challenge of getting customers back through other factors, such as service quality, or by matching Alex D's prices. This implicitly undermined Peter B's business model.

In the end, did Peter B sue Alex D for damages?

Actually, no, for the reasons outlined below.

- Alex D's behaviour in regard to the IT systems did not count as a criminal offence in the legal sense at that time.
- What actually was a criminal offence, was the theft of customer data or, rather, the use of it to gain an unfair advantage. Peter B considered his chances of suing, and came to the conclusion that, in this case, it simply wouldn't make sense. While his chances of winning a lawsuit were very good, Alex D would probably not be able to pay up, whatever the verdict.

### *Lessons learned*

**Back-up** is of critical importance to any business depending on computers to render its services. Small companies have a tendency to underestimate this while, for medium-sized to large companies, the requirement for back-up is so obvious that it doesn't need discussion. Simple measures, such as keeping the back-up at home, would already have been enough to drastically reduce recovery time.

**Legal action**. For a small company, time is of the essence. This means coming to a decision about whether it's wiser to speed up recovery as much as you can, or to spend time in

## 7: Case Studies from Small Companies

securing evidence to go to court. Bluntly, for small companies (or indeed any company) with limited resources, it makes much more sense to look forward than to engage in an investigation. When Motorola and Intel, or Oracle and SAP (initiated 2008, settled in 2011), or Microsoft and IBM fight each other in court, the potential gain outweighs the cost by orders of magnitude, and the companies are not risking their entire existence. For companies of this size, the legal minefield is not a threat to their existence, but the rewards can be extraordinary. It is this risk vs. benefit balance that allows them to pursue significant, long-running legal battles that smaller companies usually cannot afford.

For Peter B, going to court would have been costly without any likelihood of recovering damages. It is not unusual for smaller companies find themselves caught in this sort of trap.

The case illustrates a main motive of revenge combined with quite a bit of greed (opening one's own shop). The breach was facilitated, firstly, by the personality of the owner, because a slightly friendlier environment would probably have prevented it entirely and, secondly, by carelessness sadly not uncommon among small companies, which tend to focus on the next thing at hand, and sometimes overlook critical business elements, such as backup.

### Eavesdropping on faxes

While many organisations have moved beyond faxes, they remain mandatory tools in a number of industries, especially law, healthcare and finance – industries that still keep a significant amount of records in hard copy.

# 7: Case Studies from Small Companies

Somewhere in Europe, there is a company with about 15 employees, founded by an expert in the production of high quality glass lenses. Since all eligible members of the family are employed in this company, about 30% of all employees are family, making this a typical family business. They had chosen a special location for their company, right above an old mine, since the stream of cold air obtained from the mine was ideal for the slow, even cooling of the hot glass used for lenses.

The company had technology co-operation agreements with all major lens manufacturers. They were fortunate enough to gain the opportunity to bid for a consulting contract to provide their in-depth knowledge to one of the really big projects in space exploration. Months and months of discussions, meetings and travel followed until, at last, they were ready to submit a final offer. They won the contract in the end, but were absolutely stunned to discover that they had originally been underbid by an entirely unknown eastern company, which obviously knew a great deal about their offer.

It soon became clear, from an analysis of how communications had taken place, that the company's fax had been listened in to. The company was furious, of course, but decided not to pay the issue too much attention, since they had secured the contract anyway and the priorities of daily business would not leave much time for investigation.

## In-depth explanation

This case is quite an easy one, where the breach, luckily, had no consequences at all, but it shows quite clearly that, if

# 7: Case Studies from Small Companies

what you do is sophisticated enough, you will become a target, whether you expect it or not.

The company owners were completely unaware of the fact that they could be spied upon. This is normal, due to the fact that, if a company is still owned by individuals rather than being a quoted company, a sense of morality and values generally permeates the company. This ethos is something that larger corporations must work hard to achieve, and which in larger corporations can easily become lost (think of ENRON as an example). The point here is that owners with a high standard of business morals and values will be unable to imagine that others do not share these values, and this attitude is strengthened by the fact that they tend to do business with people who *do* share their values. Such people will completely refuse to believe that a breach based on industrial espionage could happen to them, even when an outsider (such as a consultant) tries to explain it to them.

It is difficult for such a company to prepare for a breach of this sort, as they would never have included espionage in their risk profile and would, furthermore, actively refuse to consider it.

This breach was, therefore, bound to occur. In this particular case though, the sophistication of the product and its high quality prevailed, despite the fact that the unfair competitor would have been cheaper.

## A stolen laptop

There is a consulting company in Germany which neatly fits the description of a small- to medium-sized business. With around 20 employees at their main location, and

## 7: Case Studies from Small Companies

subsidiaries in Austria and Switzerland, the company generates revenues of between 5 and 25 million euros annually, depending on business levels in each country. Germany usually provides the largest part of company revenue. The company was founded by its owner who, in due course, took on a second managing director, whom he trusted totally, and who had the standing of a fully accepted partner even though he was an employee.

The company focuses on SAP and IT infrastructure consulting. They put their customers' priorities first, so they tend to be a little behind in adopting technologies and new thinking (such as information security) for themselves. They can also make the same mistakes as smaller companies when fulfilling the necessities of business.

On this occasion the managing director was travelling, which was not unusual. Both the owner and the managing director would travel all around Germany, Austria and Switzerland to foster business and establish personal contact with high-ranking customer representatives. Their company laptops, of course, would be their constant companions.

At Frankfurt airport, the managing director received a call from a customer. Standing close to the gates, he put his bag down beside him to take the call. A couple of seconds later the bag, including the laptop, had disappeared. The customer database could only be accessed using a front-end, with all data being stored centrally, so it was quite secure. Contracts, draft contracts, employment agreements with temporary staff, and so on, were not. All of these were gone. The laptop, furthermore, did not have any encryption at that time, although this changed substantially after the incident. On the MD's return from his business trip, a new

## 7: Case Studies from Small Companies

order was issued: all company laptops were to be encrypted from then on, using the best software available; cost was not an issue.

In regard to the successful attack in this case, what became of the laptop is unknown, and the attacker would have found it very easy to capitalise on it; all it would have taken was to attach the laptop's drive to a different computer, and all the data on it would have been readable.

In retrospect, the company is clear that they did not suffer any losses as a consequence of this incident, but then again, there are also those losses that you will never know about.

### *In-depth explanation*

This type of case is not limited to the small company described above. It could happen to anyone travelling, regardless of company size. In a larger company, though, data would have been encrypted and the loss would not have amounted to more than the material loss of the device.

The case amply illustrates that small companies, in particular, need to learn from their mistakes, as they often lack a structured approach to information security (and therefore the avoidance of breaches). As for the managing director, he cannot really be blamed either; it is only human to be distracted and not pay full attention, and anyway, distracting people is what clever thieves aim to do. Thieves usually operate in groups of two to three; one of them distracts the victim, the second grabs or snatches whatever is available, whether a purse or a bag, and hands it over very quickly to the third thief, who then leaves the scene as soon as possible.

## 7: Case Studies from Small Companies

In this particular case, however, the theft could have easily been avoided if the MD had kept the bag between his legs while standing or sitting. This way, you will always have physical contact, and you will exert a stronger hold on the bag than if you just placed it beside your leg.

The company itself was lucky not to suffer any further damage as, had this been a targeted attack, they might well have lost business by being outbid, or by customers changing supplier. In the consultancy sector, however, a customer will not be lured away solely by price, as the business is built on trust and customers tend to stay loyal for years or even decades.

The company in this case learned the right lessons and showed this by deciding, without delay, to look after its encrypted file systems.

There are currently two methods of encryption on a laptop.

1 The entire hard disk is encrypted using a special driver that loads before the operating system boots. This very secure method can slow the machine down considerably, and you may not wish to use it on older laptops.
2 There is software, such as PGP (Pretty Good Privacy), and a number of other tools (some of them Open Source), that will allow you to choose whether to encrypt the entire hard disk, or just encrypt a file, which can then be mounted just like a hard disk. This option allows for a little more flexibility, while still as secure as the first method, since all the underlying algorithms are the same. You will also find this method easier to implement for a large number of laptops, as initial disk encryption using whole disk encryption can take up to two days for a single laptop (around 40 hours is not unusual). If you use this second approach, you

## 7: Case Studies from Small Companies

should then take care to always store your data only on the encrypted drive, otherwise you will once again be vulnerable.

Furthermore, you should understand that storage is not the only thing to worry about. If you want to tighten security, make sure also that files are deleted securely, so that no traces are left on the hard disk. A good encryption solution will usually include a tool for secure deletion of files.

# CHAPTER 8: CASE STUDIES FROM MEDIUM-SIZED COMPANIES

**A case of intrigue – the missing contract**

This case is not for the faint of heart, as it illustrates some of the rougher aspects of corporate life today.

Four medium-sized, highly regarded companies decided to join forces and brands, and combine one aspect of their activities into a new company and, thereby, a new brand. That company, henceforth called X, was established and one managing director (Y) was given full, sole decision power on all business aspects. He was given an assistant, leased to company X by one of the parent companies.

At first, all went well, and company X performed well. Suddenly, however, managing director Y developed a deep-seated desire to get rid of one of the owners by having his assistant dig up enough dirt on the person. To this day, nobody involved really understands what drove Y to this behaviour. So, after having run down company X, and after months and months of intrigue, Y was finally fired.

At this point, it turned out that it was also necessary to fire Y a second time, with all four parent companies in joint agreement. He could not just be fired from company X. Naturally, his assistant was fired, too.

All now seemed well in company X until, one day, the assistant called to claim his termination settlement in accordance with the new employment contract that Y had agreed with him. No such contract could be found, however. The assistant threatened legal action, but was willing to accept a lower sum, if the matter were promptly

## 8: Case Studies from Medium-sized Companies

settled. Since no one at X could find that contract, the cards would favour the assistant, should he go to court. Additionally, the former managing director was claiming money and benefits according to a new contract which he had obviously agreed with himself, a consequence, as it turned out later, of his being given sole decision power. Again, that contract could not be found.

So, finally, an investigator was called in and was provided with the laptops of the former director and his assistant. Although these laptops had already been reused, the investigator was able to fully recover both contracts. One minor detail turned out to be of utmost significance. Both contracts were created between Y's first and second firings.

The court of law concluded from this that, in a situation where Y was legally still employed, but had obviously lost the trust of the owners, he would not have been allowed to enter into agreements that were not in line with the owners' best interests and which were blatantly contrary to company practice. So the claims of both the former director and his assistant, totalling close to one million euros in all, were rejected in all three courts of law. Needless to say, the company was relieved after the first verdict, but it would not have taken much, maybe just a few more weeks of use of the laptops, to destroy all chances of success. Legal action in this case was spread over a period of more than two years, as the two perpetrators used every opportunity to appeal against each court decision.

# 8: Case Studies from Medium-sized Companies

## *In-depth explanation*

This case illustrates a number of information security and other related aspects. Let's start by considering the pure business aspects.

It is always a bad idea to give too much power to a single person. In this case, this was the root cause, as the new managing director was now able to run down the company, which he did for some time with the intention of placing the blame on the owners. Yes, this idea seems completely mad, but that is what happened.

The four-eyes principle is precisely about limiting power and is often extensively used in modern IT infrastructures. In business, it is usually only implemented in banks, but it is important to be aware that limiting someone's power also means limiting the amount of damage that they can do.

In this particular case, it would have been wise to work out all aspects of the organisational structure beforehand. Often, when things are going well, and the future is full of promise, we tend not to care about the more sordid details, even to the point of actively refusing to even consider what to do if things go wrong. But in this case, if the termination arrangement had been clear right from the start, it would have saved a lot of hassle and would have stopped the case from being so protracted. Going through a firing process twice is just plain embarrassing, and it was that which made this case so legally complex. As the contract in question had been entered upon between the first and second firings, there was ultimately a Supreme Court decision on what a managing director could, or could not, do under such circumstances (i.e. where he had essentially lost the trust of the owners, but was formally and legally still employed).

## 8: Case Studies from Medium-sized Companies

Now for the IT aspects. In investigations, time is of the essence. Given the peculiar circumstances of this case, it would have been wise, after firing the managing director and his assistant, not to use their laptops at all. There should have been no formatting and no reinstalling whatsoever. They should have gone straight into the safety box.

Alternatively, the company could have made a forensic image right after handover. This should have been done anyway, but it was complicated by the fact that the managing director and his assistant also had full access rights regarding their laptops, which made it quite natural that they would hand them over already reformatted.

If the managing director and the assistant had not had that level of access rights, it would have immediately aroused suspicion when they handed over their now reformatted laptops, and the investigation could have started earlier.

The head of operations at that company had first to be convinced that the data was not lost at all, because his knowledge of IT was very limited and he just couldn't image that deleted data on a PC was not, in fact, deleted. Frankly, someone who does not know about file recovery and who is unaware that, when something's deleted it is not really deleted, should get some thorough training. This is, in fact, what also happened. The head of operations underwent training and chose an outsourcing partner to help with the company IT environment, comprising a fair number of servers and clients at two different sites.

That said, convincing him took some time and, again, valuable time was lost.

# 8: Case Studies from Medium-sized Companies

## Lessons learned

As regards the business aspects, the company decided not to change much, as they considered it a fundamental expression of their core values to trust people, even with the highest levels of responsibility and power. In regard to IT, the environment was professionalised, and training was undertaken to raise senior management's understanding. Once the original business decision had been made, that was the next best thing they could have done, as it is still better to learn something than nothing.

The entire case went through three courts of law, with all the courts finally deciding in favour of the company and against the former managing director and his assistant. In this way, the company had saved about 1 million euros in total claims for a cost of 5,000 euros for forensic investigation.

Unfortunately, the relationship between the cost of investigations and the savings made is not always so favourable. It is usually safe to assume that an investigation can easily run up to 10% of the missing or stolen amount, or the amount under consideration. Once this limit is exceeded, it may be wise to reconsider how to proceed, to avoid throwing good money after bad.

## The sales manager who changed jobs

This is a case about a company which shares the world market for its product with only three other companies. The product is a highly specialised technological one which makes the life of a lot of people easier, as it deals with a medical condition that affects quite a number of people. The company was set up by a couple who got to know each other at the university where they were both studying. The husband later became a university professor, and the wife set up and ran the company as managing director.

In their early days, a sales manager was hired who performed very well. The company was putting an exceptionally high rate of 30% of revenue into research, the product got better every year, and new customers were easily acquired. Soon they were employing 30 people, then 50, then 100, mainly for production, research and patient care, as the product had to be individually fitted to the patient.

Typically for small- to medium-sized businesses, however, what the company did not take proper care of its IT systems. There was no specific regard for IT and, for some time, research staff also took care of the IT systems as a sideline. The company did not develop an understanding of the interaction between business processes and IT, nor did they care too much about their IT. Only after the company had been running for about four years was a dedicated IT manager hired. So it was not too much of a surprise to find that the researchers had made their IT life easy for themselves. Blatantly disregarding the sensitivity of their research and the need to protect it from internal and external threats, no access rights whatsoever had ever been assigned. Everybody had access to everything, which the researchers considered was the best method (sharing all information) as it greatly facilitated their work.

This situation came in very handy for the sales manager, who was, by now, a little disgruntled, as he was used to better internal organisation, and he also felt that his work was not given the appreciation it deserved. He therefore decided to change jobs, but did not know where to go. In

# 8: Case Studies from Medium-sized Companies

their limited market there were only a few options, each of which would require relocation to a different continent. Then, however, he was taken over by dark motives; he suddenly realised how he could make an offer to those other companies in the market, and make himself highly attractive as a future employee. He simply stole the data on all the newest product developments. And it was as easy as copying this data to a series of disks (USB having not yet been invented) without having to worry in the least about access rights or the monitoring of the use of such rights.

So he did that, and changed jobs. His separation from the company was quite orderly and on friendly terms, so nobody was in any way suspicious of him. The inadequacy of the IT systems only struck the owners of the company about two years later, when one of their competitors launched a product strikingly similar to their own. In the meantime they had, of course, learned where the old sales manager had gone to, but they had not worried too much. This was a big mistake.

Well, they learned their lesson, they invested in IT and in a full-time IT manager with associated staff, and they finally invested in a proper access rights scheme. On the business front, they intensified their research and soon reclaimed their number one position in the world market.

As for the sales manager, a couple of years later he did the same thing again, changing to another company and bringing some data with him. As only four companies share the world market, however, he has now more or less run out of options in this market.

# 8: Case Studies from Medium-sized Companies

## In-depth explanation

This case, too, amply illustrates some of the mistakes which plague small- and medium-sized companies.

First and foremost, IT is often not taken seriously, either in its positive aspects or its potential for harm, in cases where the company is totally occupied with itself and getting its product out into the market.

Second, even after the company has reached a stable position, it is quite difficult to undergo the restructuring and reorganisation needed to adapt the system to the necessities of grown-up company life. Some companies actually falter because they are unable to cope with their growing pains.

In this particular case, it would have been wise to professionalise internal IT much earlier, and IT should certainly not have been left as a sideline function for another department which, in any case, should under no circumstances have been a research department. Researchers tend to suffer a little from hubris as to how complicated and complex IT actually is. As soon as the company hit a level of about 20 employees, they should have taken on a dedicated IT manager. At that size, the demand for first- level support and for the upkeep of three to five servers plus network equipment usually justifies a full-time IT manager whose personnel and responsibilities will develop as the company grows.

In this case, the breach could have been prevented simply by the creation of access rights, and by great care being taken about what information was given out, and when. If all that had been done, the sales manager would have had to resort to some form of social engineering to get the latest research results. He might or might not have succeeded, but

## 8: Case Studies from Medium-sized Companies

at least there would have been another barrier to information passing into the wrong hands.

Damage to the company was considerable, but not substantial. The damage consisted of having to intensify research to regain the competitive edge and to convince the market once again of the value of its own product, since market share had dropped. At no point in time was the company in danger of entirely losing its business, but that was basically just a matter of luck, based on the extremely high degree of sophistication of the product. A company that produced commodities would not have been so lucky.

### *Lessons learned*

The main lesson to learn was obvious, and a full-time IT manager was installed soon after this incident, although it did take another five years before the IT department was fully professionalised and a good separation was in place between first-level duties, server and network administration, and IT strategy aspects. This separation should not be taken lightly, as being overwhelmed by daily work will lead even the best IT people to overlook things, or to ignore anything considered to be of lower priority.

### The project manager who became a friend, and then an enemy

This medium-sized company offers Microsoft-based technology services, and is well recognised in its national market as embodying all the best qualities that consulting and technology services represent. They are speedy in rendering services, they provide attractive pricing and maintenance schemes, and they have established an

## 8: Case Studies from Medium-sized Companies

excellent level of co-operation with their local Microsoft branch and even with Microsoft HQ.

The founder made it his principle never to work with employees, except for certain functions, such as secretaries, but to use only freelancers as consultants. He did this because he was convinced that he could save on operating costs, as well as providing his consultants with far more attractive payment schemes than would otherwise be possible. He rewarded people who were totally dedicated to their jobs and who took the initiative where necessary. After running his company for a decade, he was a little flattered when an application for a new project manager vacancy arrived, in which the applicant wrote, 'I always like to work with the best.' Yes, this was flattering; a little cheesy, though, but mostly flattering. So the man was hired and, at first, fulfilled all the founder's expectations. He was a good project manager, good with customers and staff alike, and could really drive a project. As the founder and the project manager got along very well, they eventually became friends and the founder began to think of offering him some kind of partnership.

It was just about then that things started to turn sour. First, the project manager asked for a private loan, as he had to pay off a debt because a stock market speculation of his had gone wrong. It was not a tiny sum he asked for – more than 70,000 euros, in fact. But, as a friend, he was granted the loan, and he did pay it back, albeit not on time. During this period, his performance started to drop and it almost seemed as if he was suffering from some sort of burnout or a related condition. And when the founder was actually most troubled about what to do for his friend, that friend quit his job. Coincidentally, two more people working on

## 8: Case Studies from Medium-sized Companies

the project manager's last project also left and joined a new company, set up by the ex-project manager.

Only a couple of days later, something else became clear. Some source code was gone. Parts of a new software application under development, that had cost more than 2 million euros to programme, had simply disappeared. The founder was devastated and, after giving it some thought, was clear about what to do. He needed a private investigator to see what that man, no longer referred to as a friend, was up to. He didn't want to go to court, he didn't want public exposure, he just wanted to know what was going on and, subsequently, how to counter any action that might harm his company.

The investigation was launched. The head of the investigation reported directly to the founder, and only the most trusted members of the company knew about the operation. The investigators used a team of four people to set up elaborate observation operations; they even tried to infiltrate the new company and, after about six months of investigation, they had that bit of luck that is usually required to solve a case. The former project manager, being a bit short-tempered, had one day fired his secretary from the new company. She was so shocked and angry that she simply dumped all kinds of paperwork in the paper bin and left the company. This paperwork was picked up by the investigators who, by this time, were quite desperate to report some strategically relevant news to their customer. They found they had solved the case, as the paperwork contained business plans, strategic ideas and details of customers that the company wanted to acquire, all of whom turned out to be customers of the first company.

## 8: Case Studies from Medium-sized Companies

As it was now clear to the company founder that the company which had been substantially founded by his former project manager was not a threat, he could finally put the affair to rest. The other employees who had left with the project manager couldn't stand this man's tantrums for long and, in fact, returned to the original company, where they were quickly forgiven and welcomed with open arms.

The company founder searched his soul about the whole thing for quite some time, but still found nothing he could have done to prevent these events from unfolding. He decided that he could have been more careful in choosing his friends, and that he would not, in future, be so easily taken in by flattery. Other than that, though, he had no failure to blame himself for; this was definitely the case, because it is only since 2009 that technology to prevent data leaks of this kind has been available.

### *In-depth explanation*

This case illustrates how disturbing events can become, if a person's character changes in an unexpected way. It is also, again, quite clear that an entirely trust-based culture in small and medium enterprises has a tendency to work against the company under certain circumstances.

This case is typical of an unpleasant job-changing scenario and is aggravated by the fact that the project manager did not even transgress regarding his authority or access rights. There was no collusion, no trick of any kind, no hacking, no cracking, just some plain social engineering in getting the other people to follow him. Without these people, he would not have had the slightest chance of success in establishing the new company. Still, as a project manager,

## 8: Case Studies from Medium-sized Companies

you need to be good with words, and people will sometimes be persuaded to do something against their best interest.

IT-wise, this case does not present much to learn; the lessons are basically on the business level.

Employment contracts must include NDAs that explicitly outlaw any kind of behaviour of this sort, and must contain provisions to protect the intellectual property of the company.

Where legally possible (depending on jurisdiction), any kind of engagement at a competing company should be contractually outlawed and subject to penalties for a period of one to three years. Three years is usually the maximum that can be agreed on and, in some very specialised sectors of the economy, the entire paragraph may be void because it excessively limits the future employment choices of the employee. Nevertheless, if legally available, you should make use of such stipulations.

When interviewing employees, be very careful of the overly arrogant or aggressive types. They may seem to be the right ones for the job, but they usually have, or will develop, a tendency to care for their own wealth and career more than for the common good of the company.

You may even wish to draft a list of people who, in your opinion, could put their own career first, then decide on measures to ensure that you become aware of any alarming signs that they might be planning to leave. Such signs include:

- lack of interest in their work;
- a drop in performance;
- withdrawal from company social activities;
- increased absences;

## 8: Case Studies from Medium-sized Companies

- increased absence due to illness (perhaps a pretext to hide their intentions when going to interviews with other companies).

### The lost customers – how a sales manager cost a company 10% of revenue

There's an insurance broker who specialises in a very narrow field of the insurance business. They have two significant competitors in their local market, and there is a kind of gentlemen's agreement between them not to be overly aggressive in this market. They would, for instance, never try to lure an employee away from any of the other companies, or use data acquired illegally. The company itself has roughly 100 employees and generates about 20 million euros per year in revenue.

As it happens, the company provides a very good climate for employees and nobody had ever been fired; but that was about to change.

It is significant that the insurance business is purely price driven. A company will change its insurance if it can get a better price elsewhere, as there is simply no reason not to change. Insurance has no fringe benefits to offer to customers other than to pay out insurance if required, quickly and without hassle.

So, the company was seeking a new sales manager, and a Dr X, a doctor of economics, applied for the position. In this company it was customary for applicants for key posts to also be introduced to the CEO. He did not take to Dr X at all, considering him too arrogant to fit into the company's culture, but the head of sales and the regional manager both

## 8: Case Studies from Medium-sized Companies

thought that the man was just right, and so he was eventually hired.

As it turned out, the CEO was quite right. Nobody seemed to be able to get along with this man, who quite overemphasised his title in social contact, and was very self-absorbed. Then, three months after hiring him, the unthinkable happened – the CEO received a call from one of the two competitors, who told him that Dr X had just applied to his company and had indicated that he was willing to 'bring customers with him'. Whether this referred to customers or customer data was not quite clear.

The CEO lost no time in informing the head of sales and the regional manager, and as reasons, the sales manager could not be fired on the spot for legal reasons, his contract was terminated and he was granted paid leave of absence, effective immediately. So far, so good. Everybody got on with their business, considering that the matter was closed.

But about three months later, as the year drew to a close and it came round to insurance renewal time, strange things started to happen. Customers cancelled contracts or did not renew, others called and complained bitterly about receiving calls from some foreign country and being offered better insurance rates; above all, they wondered how these people even knew about their terms. The situation was not easy and it later became clear that about 10% of revenue was lost due to customers suddenly changing their insurance provider.

It didn't take long for the CEO, the head of sales and the regional manager to work out roughly what was happening and, after some hesitation, the CEO agreed to call in private investigators. In addition, some internal research showed that Dr X had also been studying contracts that were

## 8: Case Studies from Medium-sized Companies

outside his assigned region, but which matched those of customers who had left.

For the CEO, the whole situation was new; he was used to people doing business properly and fairly and he was rather overwhelmed by the incident and its impact. He was reassured by the investigators that something could, indeed, be done about the situation, so a larger team was installed. This team consisted of a head investigator, a chief of operations (for surveillance), four more investigators to carry out the surveillance, a quality assurance investigator, and two lawyers to provide input on legal proceedings and legal options. As events unfolded, it became clear that the customers were changing to a new competitor who had just chosen to enter the local market. Further research showed that this competitor, a large European corporation, was eager to acquire market share all over Europe and had acted very aggressively in its other markets to raise its market share. That made contacting that company to discuss their code of ethics impossible.

As the lawyers were spending overtime on the case, it became clear that there was very little that could be done, because neither the stipulations for espionage nor those for unethical business practices quite fit. The strands of information were too loose to be put together to make a solid case. Then, strangely enough, the CEO of the new competitor asked to meet with the CEO of the original company, and a meeting took place.

Although the meeting itself was uneventful, what was interesting was something which the investigators came up with at the same time. On the very same day that the meeting between the two CEOs was taking place, Dr X was seen to spend four hours at the new competitor's site. While

## 8: Case Studies from Medium-sized Companies

not proving anything, this did show that the investigators' initial thinking had been going in the right direction. Furthermore, they managed to prove beyond any doubt that Dr X was, in fact, only Mr X, and that he had forged all the documents relating to his Master's degree his Ph.D.

After several months of investigation and the study of applicable laws to find better anchor points, 'Dr' X was brought to trial. He was charged with forging documents and defrauding his employer, as he had received a higher salary than would have been the case had he been only a Mr X. Unfortunately, any kind of conspiracy or agreement to steal data from the company on behalf of the new competitor could never be proven. Dr. X received a suspended prison term of six months, and was ordered to pay back an amount set by the court. He was to pay in instalments, or his suspension would be cancelled.

Finally, what the CEO wanted to achieve when the investigation had started was achieved – an end to the unpleasantness.

The CEO, however, who had to report to a supervisory board, was told by one of the supervisory board members that 'these things happen' and he was not to worry too much about it. He did, however, have to justify why he had overdrawn on the consulting budget, with the investigation and the court of law and everything else. Eventually, his explanations were accepted but the supervisory board did not really enter any kind of learning curve on these matters.

### *In-depth explanation*

This case was particularly distasteful, and it illustrates several aspects in excellent detail.

## 8: Case Studies from Medium-sized Companies

If your business is almost entirely based on price, your pricing structure becomes your most important asset and needs to be protected accordingly.

If you have to deal with an aggressive new competitor who is prepared to use illegal means, your risk profile is further aggravated. Your level of care should increase with your risk profile.

Follow your instincts. The CEO was absolutely right in his opinion of the sales manager, but did not dare overrule his head of sales and regional manager, as the company had (and still has) a very positive, cooperative climate. Given the actual damage done and the general potential for sales people to do damage in a price-driven business, it would have been wiser for the CEO to overrule his staff and maybe risk them being grumpy for a while.

In this company, software for data leakage prevention would certainly have avoided the breach entirely, with the sole exception of those customers the sales manager was assigned to. He would not have been able to copy the details of customers who were not in his domain. That said, it should be clearly stated that no working data leakage prevention solution existed at the time of this incident, so we are talking with the benefit of hindsight. Of course, that should not stop you, as you read this, from seriously considering data leakage prevention products for your company environment.

Although the company was already quite sizeable, the access rights system was based too heavily on trust, rather than on the need-to-know principle. It may well demand a certain effort to explain to your staff that a thoroughly designed and implemented access rights structure is no sign of mistrust, but it is worth the effort, given that, in this case,

## 8: Case Studies from Medium-sized Companies

it would have helped to prevent at least some aspects of the damage.

The case also illustrates that lack of information security awareness does not stop at the top. In this case, the responsible member of the supervisory board showed no awareness whatsoever, and even downplayed the damage, which amounted to about 10% of yearly revenue. This could be understood as being motivated by an instinct for self-protection, because board members and supervisory board members tend to be very sensitive about issues of liability, but this blatant misunderstanding of the underlying dangers is quite stunning.

This case also makes a point in showing that the legal aspects of such a situation can be absolutely mind-boggling. The poor legal result can be explained along the following lines.

- The sales manager did not 'spy' on the company in the legal sense, as that would have necessitated some contact and agreement on spying between the sales manager and the aggressive competitor. There was only a slight chance of proving such an agreement and prior contact.
- The sales manager did not transgress his powers, because, based on the access rights system in place, he could access all data of all customers countrywide, even those not in his work domain.
- On the subject of unethical business practices, it was not sufficiently proven that there was a direct link between the sales manager, the foreign insurance trader who kept calling customers, and the aggressive new competitor. The items of evidence available were just a little too weak. The best evidence could have been gained from a former employee of the new competitor, who had quit

## 8: Case Studies from Medium-sized Companies

because he found their new way of acquiring customers too unethical. Unfortunately, he did not wish to talk about it, far less appear in court as a witness.

This last point also illustrates the legal culture of that country, in which companies are reluctant to sue one another. That has its benefits, but in this case the company, simply by not wishing to follow through, did not make use of the opportunity to gain full damage recovery, albeit through a lengthy judicial process. Having the testimony of the unwilling former employee would have made all the difference between a speculative case and one that was already almost won by the time it reached court.

### *Lessons learned*

The company certainly tightened its access rights system to separate the regional business domains but, first and foremost, it strengthened its recruitment process, which now includes the basic screening of all candidates.

### The flood – how not to learn about risk management

In the early 2000s, a certain country was hit by a severe flood. The flood was so bad that a national emergency was declared, and the military and emergency sectors, public and voluntary, spent a lot of time getting the floods under control. Parts of the country were simply devastated. And then, there was company X.

Company X was an industrial company working in the automotive sector and during the flood it was simply washed away. Of course, its IT was also washed away and, having no disaster recovery plan and no kind of business

# 8: Case Studies from Medium-sized Companies

continuity planning, the company ground to a halt at all levels. As if that was not bad enough, 200 jobs were at stake, and it was vital that production should be resumed as soon as possible, as the larger companies which were company X's customers did not have a lot of patience. So, under extreme pressure, the company's production capability was restored and its IT systems renewed, mainly by the purchase of completely new equipment and the reinstallation of everything including servers, ERP system and client PCs. Fortunately for the company, the entire IT side of things was fully funded by the local state government, who deemed that the 200 jobs were definitely worth saving.

So far so good, but the punch line in this simplest of stories is that, some months later, the owner of the company was approached by large IT-sector company which wanted to talk to him about risk management. When they asked him whether or not he wanted to do anything about it, his answer became instant, nationwide, consulting business lore. What he actually said was, "Why should I? Next time something happens, the state will just pay again!"

I have to admire this man for his blind trust in a completely unpredictable outcome of an even more unpredictable situation.

## *In-depth explanation*

This case includes several points deserving detailed explanation.

Even though floods were considered unlikely in that country, they should not have been omitted from a risk analysis and from company thinking. You do not

## 8: Case Studies from Medium-sized Companies

necessarily have to consider a flood, but you should, from time to time, ask yourself, 'Which events could seriously harm my business or bring my company to a standstill?' If you ask yourself this question and consider the answers thoroughly, you are performing a good risk / business continuity analysis or at least venturing into that terrain.

In risk analysis terms, the case shows the consequences of not having considered risk at all. It is doubtful whether floods would even have been considered, given that this flood was bigger than a 100-year flood scenario, but at least something might have struck the company. It would most probably have been considered as an event causing extreme damage, but with a very low probability, therefore yielding only a middle-to-low priority result as calculated by old-style risk analysis.

The case further illustrates that although miracles happen (the state paying for the infrastructure), common sense dictates that this cannot be taken for granted, and by no means justifies ignoring one's risk profile.

Whatever his motive was in being so rude to the consultants from the IT company, maybe the owner chose his words as he did because he wanted to get rid of them. On the other hand, taken at face value, it just illustrates that there's no cure for stupidity.

Given the all-powerful nature of medium-sized company owners, that is also the end of the story. No lesson was learned.

Medium-sized companies in the automotive sector tend to learn very fast once their customers ask for something, such as enhanced information security measures. As of 2014, the automotive sector has successfully adopted its own version

## 8: Case Studies from Medium-sized Companies

of ISO27001 and, while this has not yet arrived at all levels of the supply chain, Tier 1 and Tier 2 suppliers (those who assemble entire cars and those who provide essential parts) have, by now, been certified.

The company in this case will probably have to learn the hard way when it is offered a choice by its customers: do something or lose business.

# CHAPTER 9: CASE STUDIES FROM LARGE CORPORATIONS

## Who wants my data? – a case of data theft

There's a company which does 100% of its business online. It specialises in providing online services, so its IT systems and their security are of considerable importance. As any big company (4,000+ employees, several sites and branches worldwide) would do, they have a PR department that also follows up on Internet gossip, on what is going on in the chat rooms provided by the company, and in relevant online forums. This turned out to be a very wise move as, one lovely July day, a message popped up in one of these forums which froze the blood of the head of PR.

The message read: *Do you want to start your own online services company? – Customer contact list for sale – full details, names, addresses, CC info.*

So the head of PR did what he was supposed to do in such cases, and called up the head of security, who was fortunate enough to have held that position only for a couple of months; he certainly would not have wanted to be held responsible for what had happened. He lost no time in getting hold of the message and all available details then, without further ado, turned to an investigator for assistance. On the very same day, a team was assembled which consisted of:

- a head of investigation, bearing full responsibility for everything that happened as part of the investigation;

## 9: Case Studies from Large Corporations

- a head of operations, in charge of all tactical matters such as carrying out observations and acquiring information;
- a quality assurance investigator who would review all documents and provide feedback on all planned steps;
- a team with a variable number of members to perform surveillance. In this case, the maximum number of agents used was six;
- a lawyer who would provide input on legal matters and on how these could be used should the case go to court.

The team started its work immediately, and the head of security also put his own people to work on some technical aspects, in close co-ordination with the investigation team.

One of the first things they found out was through quite a piece of luck. The original message in the Internet forum contained a link to what seemed to be a project belonging to the writer. They visited the link and took a simple step, once they thought of it; namely, looking at the source code of this web page. This revealed something very interesting – a file path containing a name, since the page had obviously been created on Microsoft® Windows® equipment and uploaded from the user's personal profile folder. So there it was: a name.

In parallel, fake negotiations were entered into with the writer who, step by step, revealed more details about himself. The goal of such negotiations is always the same: first, establish as much trust as needed (as fake buyer) to allow you to be the one who calls the shots. Then get the perpetrator to meet in person for a handover of some sample data. Using this sample data, you can find out whether the sale is actually based on real data, pointing to a severe breach, or whether the sale is entirely fake.

## 9: Case Studies from Large Corporations

Unfortunately, as the victim, you almost always have to take this first step and spend some money to find out whether or not you are really under threat. There is not much else you can do at this stage.

Once it turns out that the data is not fake, you would establish contact with the police, let them take the lead, and work towards some personal handover of the entire dataset, with the police arresting the criminals on handover.

In this case, things turned out to be pretty straightforward. From the fake negotiations and additional research, it became clear that the suspect was living in the country where the company had its headquarters, which would make legal follow-ups a lot easier. The investigation team was able to come up with a name, an address, a photo and a date of birth. The perpetrator was only 14½ years old, which made him legally old enough to face criminal proceedings. And on top of it all, when contact was established with the police, it turned out that this child had already had one run-in with the law for fraudulent Internet activity.

The data, however, turned out to be authentic and that was the scary part.

As the case progressed, it turned out that the child was conducting all this activity, using a laptop, from where the family was on holiday in Greece. The investigators now had to find out when they would return, and where they would be coming back to. There were several possibilities, as the parents were divorced and the grandparents ran a small country hotel. This meant that a total of three surveillance teams was needed to locate them correctly.

## 9: Case Studies from Large Corporations

You can image the surprise of the parents as they returned from their holiday when the police, notified by the surveillance team, raided them and impounded all computer hardware that could be found, including the laptop and additional hard disks.

As the child showed some remorse, he agreed to be interviewed with his father present, then reported all the sordid details to the investigators. And here the case ran dry again, as the child was only a dealer, and could not reveal much contact information about those behind the theft.

Legally, the child was only charged with fraud, as he had advertised that he was in possession of millions of customer records while, in fact, he only had about 10,000. He was let off lightly, received a suspended sentence and, as media reports showed some years later, all his later business ideas were legitimate ones.

As for the data theft, that was the tricky bit. Further research showed that the original company had bought another company, in a European country, just a couple of months previously, and that that was where the theft had occurred.

The best explanation they could come up with of what had happened went as follows:

- Their new acquisition had wanted to shut down a couple of services and servers, and their idea of shutting down the devices was simply to take them out of DNS, but leave them connected while not doing any further maintenance on them.
- Over a period of four months, the attacker then successfully exploited an OS vulnerability to run a SQL injection attack and get hold of the customer records.

## 9: Case Studies from Large Corporations

- An estimated 4 million records were lost, including user passwords, but luckily no payment details such as credit card information.

Naturally, some organisational changes were made to the new subsidiary company and a tighter hold was exerted on all change management procedures inside that company.

Furthermore, the company had all user passwords changed and, luckily, no abuse was reported by users.

The stolen list, however, is still at large, though it is mostly useless. The physical addresses of the customers from the list were used at least once, when the chief executive of one company received an advertisement from a new and totally unknown competitor, in which his address was spelt exactly as in the company's database, including all spelling mistakes.

This all served as a giant wake-up call about the realities of doing Internet-related business today. The company has not only strengthened its security since then, it has also used this incident to establish standard procedures on how to deal with such cases in the future.

### *In-depth explanation*

The case presented here is quite typical of what can happen to a big corporation. It also highlights the fact that one of the main groups of perpetrators of computer crime today consists of gifted individuals (generally male) aged between 14 and 25, who have nothing better to do with their time. It also shows that companies sometimes make it much too easy for such people to succeed, landing themselves with heavy investigational and recovery costs.

## 9: Case Studies from Large Corporations

The case shows that a vigilant PR department can be a very good first line of defence in actually detecting a breach. Had it not been for the PR department and its standard routine of reading relevant forums, the breach might have remained unnoticed for much longer. If you belong to a big company, you should adopt this practice, though chances are that your PR department is already doing so.

It is essential that a clear reporting structure exists. It does not have to be fully formalised, though ideally it ought to be. It is absolutely fundamental to information security awareness that people know where to go to report an incident. The head of PR did just the right thing in reporting this incident to the head of security right away, which is the next important thing: report immediately, not as soon as possible.

The investigation team in this case might seem large, but its size and composition are quite typical for such cases. It is appropriate in dimension and scope and will usually only vary in the number of field agents used. Such a team comes at a cost of approximately 10,000 euros per day, but an investigation is characterised by intense phases of activity, followed by phases where nothing needs to be done, so the actual cost will always depend on the intensity of the case and its characteristics. The figure presented is more a rule of thumb.

Quality management is also necessary. Investigations do not forgive mistakes, so having an additional, senior and experienced investigator on board, who provides input on all plans and feedback on all actions taken can be tremendously important. Be aware, though, that these two qualities (senior and experienced) do not necessarily come in one package, and that the person you look for should

## 9: Case Studies from Large Corporations

ideally be in their 50s, having served in progressively more responsible job functions, preferably with an economic crime unit.

In cases like this, the best chance of success always comes from direct contact with the perpetrator. The investigators, therefore, need to be skilled in social engineering and able to take control of the perpetrator and steer them through the proceedings. The younger and less hardened the person is, the more easily this will work, but even hardened criminals have weak spots or vulnerabilities that can be exploited during negotiations to make them steerable.

It is also important to have all relevant staff needed for the case on heightened alert, and on stand-by if necessary. In this particular case, all data verifications were made at a different site, so the people had to be informed and put on stand-by. This can become more complicated if teams are working across different time zones, though that was not the case here.

Luck was on the side of the company in this case, as the main perpetrator was located in the same country. That simplifies the whole investigation and the case by orders of magnitude as most of our judicial systems have not yet adapted to the scenarios of cyber crime, where national borders do not really have a meaning. In Europe, for example, it will take Europol (the co-ordination office of the EU's police forces) about two weeks to follow up on a case, which is totally useless in relation to the speed with which the perpetrators work. It is, therefore, not in any way sarcastic to state that a good investigation company with an extensive international network will be able to serve you better than the police could.

## 9: Case Studies from Large Corporations

The root cause of this incident was the acquisition of the other company, coupled with the slightly negligent way in which control was taken over. Of course, all mergers need time for their full potential and their synergies to appear, and this process can take three to five years. Under no circumstances, though, should a security gap of such magnitude be the result of a merger. The company should have exerted tight control over the acquisition's IT processes and enforced this control from Day One of the merger. The buying company was in a better position as regards process maturity, so it was hard to understand why the other company was granted such a long leash.

### Lessons learned

As for lessons learned, the company did the best it possibly could to respond to the wake-up call it received. While it was tedious to initiate this investigation, the whole process of dealing with real and potential breaches was revised and brought to a professional level. The case also emphasised how important it was to exert tighter control on the acquired company, and that, too, was swiftly accomplished.

As is typical for larger companies, if they want to learn their lesson, they will, and with the proper drivers in place (in this case the head of security and the COO) changes will be speedily made.

### Who wants my data? – a more complicated case

This case happened at the same company as Case 1, sometime after that case was concluded. There had been no new breach, but the data was still in the wild and, until you

## 9: Case Studies from Large Corporations

have checked some of the data, you cannot tell whether there is a new breach or not.

At the beginning, this case was much the same as Case 1. This time someone had approached the call centre of a competitor in Panama, leaving a message for the head of marketing in which they offered to sell data. The head of marketing and the CEO of that company did not want to get involved in that sort of business and, through two middlemen, contacted the company. As contact between the companies was established, the investigators were in close contact with this other company and were even allowed to act under false identities taken from that company.

This time, therefore, the company had a good starting point since many of the procedures they needed to apply had already been field-tested, and close contact had been established with the company to which the data had been offered.

So the investigation team was assembled once again, but it soon became clear that things were going to be a little more complicated this time.

The perpetrator (or at least the vendor) was located in another European country. That made the case infinitely more difficult, as European inter-police co-operation has not been designed to work really fast, particularly not on cases that, although they may harm a company, are not of real public interest. It therefore became clear quite soon that the good police ties which had been established could only be used if, in the course of the investigation, the perpetrator(s) could be lured to the home country and arrested there.

## 9: Case Studies from Large Corporations

For the moment, however, all communication was based on Internet chats using Skype. This had one big advantage: if you use Skype, all chats (the typed chat, not the telephone conversations) are recorded and you can save them for later use in court; by installing additional software you can record telephone conversations as well.

So, negotiations were begun, and dragged on for almost a two weeks until a first sample of data was to be made available by the seller. Transfer of this was, however, a problem. The investigators were very keen not to give up their fake identity, so they did not want to make any kind of online payment to the seller. The seller wanted, at first, to meet on some remote island in the middle of the Bothnian Sea. They managed to convince him to meet them in another European country, which meant that the investigation team had to fly to that country with only a couple of hours' notice. A price of about 5,000 euro was agreed, to be handed over in cash and, as preparations were very rushed, the money had to be counted and registered on the plane, which earned them some odd looks from the stewardesses. Registering the money means taking down all the numbers of the notes, so as to be able to identify them later on. In this particular case it turned out not to be useful, but you can never be sure.

On arrival, one investigator was to meet with the vendor, while the other would try to secretly get a few photos of the perpetrator.

The meeting took place at the airport and, once again, the perpetrator turned out to be a youth, about 20 years old, who had just finished school and was waiting to do his military service. He had already established quite an online

## 9: Case Studies from Large Corporations

contact network, and further traces of the data led to Canada, which made the investigation all the more difficult.

The investigator was, as is standard practice, recording everything that was said and, at one point, the perpetrator said something very important to the whole direction of the investigation. His words were, "I am doing a lot of business right now, including black business". That statement would have been worth a great deal in a court of law as it proved something very important: that he knew that his actions were illegal and was determined to carry on. This could gain him a significant prison sentence later on.

Within a short time, an envelope of money was exchanged for a USB stick containing data samples. The readability of the stick was verified on the spot and the parties went their separate ways.

Back at home, a team of four people spent some time analysing the data and they found that, while it was authentic, it was also old, although some records seemed to be brand new. There were only a few of these, though, and they could well have come from other sources, as having affiliates and partners sharing links is very important to raise business in the online world. The youth was by now known to be in contact with such affiliates.

So what was purchased was basically just junk, and did not point at all to a new leak. That was the good news.

Negotiations then dragged on for some time, until it was decided with the customer that the best and most cost-effective move was now to drop the camouflage and give the vendor a choice: co-operate and tell us all you know, or be prosecuted. To this end, an elaborate trap was designed for the youth and his suspected partner (the Canadian)

## 9: Case Studies from Large Corporations

which involved inviting them to come to the home country for a gala where the entire data set would be handed over at a price of one million euros. Since the data had checked out as valid, at least the perpetrators could then be arrested on the spot for fraud.

The trap was never carried out. The following reasons clearly illustrate the intricacies of such investigations.

The police unit, with which an excellent working relationship was established, was unable to assist as the sum involved would automatically require special forces to be brought into the picture. The main result of that would have been that the operation would almost certainly not have remained secret. The customer did not want that at all, since even though this was just a follow-up case it would have been hard to explain to the public.

The customer did not wish to provide the one million euros, for fear that the sum might be lost. The chances of that were absolutely minimal, but one million is quite a lot of money, so the investigating team understood their reticence.

Once the trap had been called off, what remained was the ultimatum already described. This approach usually works when applied to someone who is not a hardened criminal, and it worked in this case, too. The youth's co-operation was secured and he was invited to headquarters for a long talk about the whole case and to tie up the remaining loose ends. To ensure that he did not suddenly drop out of the agreement (that if he talked, the charges would be dropped) he was picked up in a Northern European country and accompanied to headquarters. Someone even stayed in the same hotel, just to make sure that he would not suddenly decide not to co-operate.

# 9: Case Studies from Large Corporations

The talk produced good results and some loose ends were dealt with. The youth was let off, which led to some dispute within the investigation team, but it was ultimately decided that getting closer to the truth was worth more than could be gained by engaging in an even lengthier investigation including the police forces of several countries, especially since no new threat existed.

So, finally, dozens of pages of printed Internet chat, technical evaluations, meeting reports and decisions went to where they belonged – in the archives.

## *In-depth explanation*

This case is quite similar to the first one except for one essential difference: the international scope. As long as everything (the company, the breach, the perpetrator) stays in the same country, dealing with a breach is easy. It is easy to establish contact with the police, to co-operate and to close in on the perpetrator, with the cost being that of the investigators used. In other words, it is controllable and not excessive. But when the case becomes international things can become infinitely more complicated and the company may face new challenges, having to deal with jurisdictions in which cyber crime simply does not exist or countries where corruption is rampant and the system will usually work against you.

In this particular case the following countries were involved:

- Panama: the site where the crime became apparent.
- USA: the country where the competing company had its headquarters.

## 9: Case Studies from Large Corporations

- Costa Rica: the country where a trace of the original perpetrator (not the vendor) was leading.
- Europe: the location of the victim company.
- A different European country: the location of the perpetrator (where he had his permanent address).
- Yet another European country: where the first exchange of money against sample data took place.

It is not at all easy to decide where it would make sense to go, where to establish surveillance operations, and so on. Once again, the key in conducting the investigation was social engineering against the perpetrator (or, in this case, the vendor) to gain as much information as possible in order to develop a plausible scenario of the root cause of the breach, and to find substantial evidence to awaken the interest of the authorities. In this case, the fact that the US was remotely involved would have made things easier, as the US, like Britain, is known to follow up thoroughly on cyber crime; but in the course of the investigation, the idea of filing a criminal complaint in the US was dismissed for purely practical reasons. This also highlights the fact that the legal costs of even evaluating the best way to proceed may outrun the cost of the operational aspects of an investigation. This diverts the whole process into a series of business decisions about cost, thereby short changing the investigation.

The reader should also remember that this case was made easier by the fact that it was a sort of follow-up to the first one. This meant that it quite soon became clear, after the first exchange had taken place and data had been evaluated, that the case was not a very serious one. In practice, you will have to treat each alleged or presumed breach with full priority until it is clear whether you have suffered a breach.

## 9: Case Studies from Large Corporations

It is important to emphasise that whenever negotiations take place you must have a means of recording them. You should use Skype for text chats, as Skype will store chats for at least 30 days. You can also use Skype for telephone chats together with a product called Pamela Call Recorder to record the call. Once you have stored a chat, be sure to save it to some write-protected media, such as a DVD or CD, and protect it with an MD5 hash code, to be able to prove that the recording has not been altered in any way since it was made.

The case also illustrates that, for reasons of cost, private investigations are usually limited in the number of people that can be employed. Going to another country to meet the vendor for the first time, using only two investigators, and having to use inferior mobile recording equipment (due to short notice) was less than optimal. If you can make good use of even the worst equipment available, however, you will still come up with an acceptable result. In this case the pictures taken were not very good, because nobody could be prepared for the location and circumstances, but the sound recording was excellent which helped a great deal in moving the case along.

The case also shows that companies need clear guidance if they are inexperienced in investigations. In this case the investigators were incredibly frustrated when, having set an enormously elaborate trap which could have helped them arrest the seller and the actual cracker, they finally had to let go of it; however, the company which owns the investigation has the undisputed right to change its directions, no matter how unpleasant this may be. The investigators must have a firm hand in coming up with a strategy and then employing the tactics that have been decided upon. If matters such as a trap need to be discussed,

## 9: Case Studies from Large Corporations

the same firm hand is used when presenting and explaining details of the matter, but investigators must still be prepared to go along with the company's ultimate decision.

Please note that the ultimatum described here only worked because the vendor was not a hardened criminal, and did not want to go to prison. When dealing with organised crime or hardened individuals, it will be much more complicated to achieve success. If organised crime is involved the police should be brought in anyway, as such cases can turn out to be too hot for even the most experienced private investigators to handle and the reward is usually not consistent with the level of risk incurred. In the case of the hardened criminal, negotiations will be protracted, and you will need to accept that a much higher level of technical sophistication will be needed to get a firm handle on the perpetrator.

Ideally, an investigation will succeed up to the point where the perpetrator can be delivered to the police, but the police will usually take over at any point if you wish them to do so. They will then take the case entirely out of your hands, which may, of course, be an undesired side effect.

Finally, the case illustrates that, as we are all human, sometimes giving somebody, even a perpetrator, a second chance is well worth it. In this case the youth, once he returned from doing his military service, started to work for one of the companies involved and was eager to prove himself, which turned him into a respectable, efficient employee. He has also helped in uncovering a number of other schemes, and has become a valuable asset in these cases. He may not be a Kevin Mitnick – technically, he certainly is not – but sometimes, as a company, you can benefit from bringing souls back to the side of

## 9: Case Studies from Large Corporations

righteousness. You need to be careful when you make this sort of decision, though. If the youth had already had a criminal conviction, then it would not have been prudent to have hired him.

### Hard disk for sale – beware of your contractors

This case was a public one, and has been reported in the media. It provides an excellent illustration of some of the more delicate aspects of information security management.

In a certain Ministry of Economics in one European country, everyone was perfectly content. The ministry was in good shape in information security terms and had even implemented some very new methods of securing data. Their paper and disks were shredded when they were no longer needed, and this was all taken care of by a trusted contractor, renowned throughout the country for its trustworthiness.

One day, however, things changed dramatically. Someone – it is not known who – discovered that he could make a very interesting purchase on eBay: a disk, openly advertised as containing data from this Ministry of Economics. The vendor should, of course, have known that if this was one sale the sale would not work out. Instead of selling to some gullible person, the vendor – who worked for the famously 'trustworthy' shredding contractor – was arrested and the whole thing became public knowledge through the media, which always likes a good story. The leak occurred at the shredding company and one of its employees was the vendor.

## 9: Case Studies from Large Corporations

Ultimately, the contract with the shredding company was terminated and the employee was fired. Peace was restored – or was it?

***In-depth explanation***

This case illustrates one especially delicate point in information security – how to deal with one's contractors. Even as a really large corporation or, as in this case, a ministry, you will find yourself in a position where you cannot handle all aspects of information security yourself. This applies particularly to recycling and disposing of equipment. Only the military is known to cover these aspects themselves, but we mere mortals usually rely on contractors to perform the job.

This case clearly shows that you can do everything right and still suffer a breach, as the chain of damage will not stop at the contractor itself. The stolen disk and its intended sale directly affected the customer, with the contractor being more of an indirect victim, as it suffered the ministry's anger and subsequent termination of contract. That termination of contract, however, could not provide an assurance that such a thing would not happen with the next contractor, as the root cause was simply the behaviour of the individual employee. ISO27001 offers a number of essential remedies for this situation.

Your contract with your service provider needs to be as tight as it can be. You should not be afraid to state all expectations in ample detail. A typical ITIL®-based outsourcing contract can easily contain 1,000 pages of stipulations, so a contract on disposal may contain 10 to 20 pages of detailed regulations.

## 9: Case Studies from Large Corporations

You should reserve the right to audit the contractor and you should make use of that right. You should also be strict in being transparent about its protocol and findings while carrying out the audit. In this way, you will demonstrate to the employees of the contractor that you are serious about your business.

You should define contractual penalties, for the case where deviations from the agreed procedures are found. You do not necessarily have to invoke these, but they should be there to make clear the importance of your message.

Rather unconventionally, you may insist that your contractor perform certain key actions, such as background checking on hires sent to your premises, and frequent changes of personnel.

In the above case, a good process which would have made the breach impossible would have been to have destroyed or damaged the disks before handing them over to the contractor. At its simplest, you can always drill through a hard disk and thereby render it unusable except by highly specialised labs. Physical damage or demagnetisation (degaussing) are essentially the best ways to protect information remaining on a disk. Alternatively, the ministry could have securely erased all data first, which is certainly an action that could reasonably be expected of them. While secure erasing is very time consuming, it can be done without manual intervention, and only depends on setting up an appropriate 'production line' where computers perform the erasures 24x7.

# 9: Case Studies from Large Corporations

## Unauthorised domain links – it is easy to harm a company's reputation

This case is about a breach, not so much of confidentiality, as of trust. It does, however, illustrate how difficult it can be to remove from the web material that can damage your reputation; in this case it was not even material, but just a mere link.

Companies who do online business often have very elaborate schemes of affiliation whereby the affiliates can make money or receive other benefits for bringing web traffic and, therefore, customers, to the company. One particular affiliate, however, had a very strange idea about what he could do to raise money.

Let's say the company in question is called <u>www.some-online-company.com</u>. This is the link that will pop up on affiliates' websites, with the aim that people get curious about the business and check out the company website. This is what the affiliate did, in a perfectly legal way, and he was actually one of the more successful affiliates in bringing traffic to the company.

One day, however, someone in PR noticed that an Internet domain existed which was called something like <u>www.whos-the-biggest-fraud.com</u>. Now this website, when surfed to, would immediately redirect people to the company website of <u>www.some-online-company.com</u>. In this way, the affiliate could increase his income by directing traffic to the company through his other (legal) links and by getting even those people sceptical of the company to go to the company's website, if they used this defamatory link; quite clever, indeed.

## 9: Case Studies from Large Corporations

So, once this was known, a single investigator was charged with finding out the identity of this person, and with discovering as much information as was needed to close down the site. The investigation brought to light a number of facts:

- The website itself was hosted in Germany. The German ISP hosting it was quite surprised about the site, but did not want to co-operate without a court order, even for just handing out owner information, which is usually in the public domain anyway. After some robust discussions, however, they were brought to at least confirming the owner's details, which the investigator had procured through other channels.
- The investigator had been lucky in being able to discover other channels through which information on the domain owner could be obtained. That information was verified several times and was found to be correct and valid.

The case was then handed back to the company and their affiliates department, as they were the best people to make a choice on how to proceed.

In the end, it turned out that there was no way to deliver letters to the domain owner, as he was already in prison, serving a sentence for tax fraud. Furthermore, as his legal affiliate activities were bringing in plentiful hits, terminating his contract was not an option the company wanted to follow up.

That domain exists to this day, and maybe the company will have to wait until their affiliate gets out of prison to give him a really good talking to.

The potential legal case here would be based on defamation and on unethical business conduct, as the domain owner

## 9: Case Studies from Large Corporations

would be directly profiting from having people reroute to the company website through the defamatory site.

**In-depth explanation**

This case does have some funny aspects, as you would probably not suspect your perpetrator to already be in jail. Practically speaking, however, it made dealing with it all the more difficult, as there was simply no means of delivering a legal brief. It could have been managed once it had become clear where this person was imprisoned, but the company didn't want to go to those lengths.

In addition, the entire case came down to quite a difficult business decision, as the domain owner was bringing much desired traffic to the company's site, while, at the same time, abusing that very business model to make an additional profit at the company's expense. So the main decision became whether to sever ties with this person, and they decided not to do so.

The investigation was a milk run, executed by one single investigator who was successful in getting the true identity of the person and in securing enough cooperation from the uncooperative domain provider to verify the results of prior research. The only technical tools used were the standard Microsoft® Windows® and UNIX tools used to get domain name information from the WhoIs service which all Internet service providers use to store domain owner information.

The case, however, illustrates very well how easy it is to harm a company, and how it may not be so easy to define that harm legally, as all it consisted of was the link to the company's website. There was also a risk of going to

## 9: Case Studies from Large Corporations

court without sufficient certainty of conviction and cost recovery.

It needs to be noted that, strictly speaking, the 'breach' (in this case an incident rather than a breach), has not been fully dealt with, neither has it been resolved. It does show, however, what kind of risk-related business decisions can be required from companies whose business exists entirely online.

### The trusted guard who was not

This case once more illustrates how important it is:

- to choose one's contractors carefully;
- for these contractors to choose their personnel carefully;
- to have a secure IT environment.

There is a certain defence sector company which one would expect to take their security extremely seriously, given all the requirements made upon them, largely by the governments who are their main customers. Even nowadays, however, it is still a challenge for any company to get the whole chain of trust right, as this case shows.

The company relied on a third-party service provider for guard and gate services to the company's premises, and it was contractually agreed that the guards would change every now and then, usually after about six months. So, in the middle of the year, a new guard was posted to the premises. Had the contracting company run even the most basic criminal background check, they would have noticed that this individual already had one conviction for computer-based fraud. The guard, obviously, did well to hide his true nature and non-job-related talents. For the next couple of months, he served politely and quietly, courteously and charmingly, and it was felt that he was doing the job pretty well.

Unnoticed, however, he began to connect his own laptop to the company network which, frankly, should never have worked in the first place. Exploiting further weaknesses in the IT infrastructure of the company, along with predictable passwords for network equipment, he managed to get access to the CFO's network traffic and, with a little more effort, he discovered a number of online banking IDs, PINs and some transaction numbers that the CFO exchanged with his staff, and which had, therefore, not yet been used.

So, the final act began, and the guard initiated some bank transfers with the stolen data, to several accounts, so that it would not be immediately clear where the payments were going. The payments were substantial, but not really high enough to arouse suspicion.

What did alert the CFO, however, was the fact that these transfers took place on a Friday, and he knew that he never made bank transfers on a Friday. That simple fact ignited the case which was handed over to the police without any further ado. The guard was arrested and convicted once more, the contract with the contractor was terminated and an IT manager was fired. The company had decided on a full clean-up.

Note that what the company did is not to be taken for granted. In a similar case recently, the contracting company offered to pay for the damage, and simply fired the guard without any further criminal proceedings. In that case, it was deemed best to preserve a low public profile, and not to alert the media of anything that could become a good story by reporting the case to the police.

# 9: Case Studies from Large Corporations

## In-depth explanation

This case, once more, highlights the risks inherent in third-party outsourcing, but, in this case, the obvious mistakes and errors made are staggering and blatant. This is a defence sector company, so security should be at its best, not somewhere between medium and poor. In view of that one fact, the eventual firing of the IT manager was fully justified.

The security company providing the guard made an essential and basically unforgiveable mistake in not checking his background. That was strange, as they would normally have checked. Particularly with customers in this sort of sector, you should not allow the least element of carelessness; there should be absolutely no negligence.

The company made several IT-related mistakes. One was to use easy-to-guess passwords for its network equipment, which enabled the guard to monitor the CFO's network connection, once he had found out which network ports to monitor. The second error was not to monitor usage of administrative commands on its network equipment – which could easily have been done. Thirdly, and most importantly, the guards should never have been able to attach their own equipment to the network – that is just unforgiveable. They should have been provided with company-issued PCs and, yes, it would make sense to allow them to surf the Web, as guard duty can be very boring sometimes, and this would actually help keep spirits and vigilance up, if used responsibly. Furthermore, it is really easy today, with even the most inexpensive network equipment, to configure it in such a way that no other devices than those specified can be attached. That one simple provision could have prevented the entire incident.

## 9: Case Studies from Large Corporations

The company was simply lucky that the CFO was able to realise so quickly that there had been a breach. Had the guard been more careful, the breach might have remained unnoticed for long enough for him to move to another job.

This case is typical of most breach scenarios, where one essential vulnerability (the actual hiring of the guard based on incomplete information) was aggravated by a company's own shortcomings and resulted in quite a severe incident. Not all incidents can be as easily resolved as this one was.

**Insider badmouthing**

This next case serves to illustrate the difficulties of investigating company insiders who share their knowledge (or some of it) through online forums.

Take, for instance, an online services company which is also traded on the international stock market. Who knows what about the company's figures, and when, is a matter not to be taken lightly in view of insider trading regulations. Furthermore, the company's reputation is taken very seriously, and some people's only business in the PR department is to monitor relevant online forums for news and reports on the company.

On one occasion, they came across several entries in a stockholder forum where one member was ranting about the company, making defamatory comments, and generally writing very bad things about the company. While this would all come under the freedom of speech regulations (except for the defamatory parts), one sentence alerted the company: "I know, because I work there." This set alarm bells ringing, and the PR department notified the head of security who engaged an investigator to find out all

## 9: Case Studies from Large Corporations

there was to discover. The case was not assigned highest priority, though.

As it turns out, the identity of the writer was quite well hidden and no conventional, or even less conventional, means were successful in finding the person. The ultimate option, an elaborate social engineering scheme, by which their trust was to be gained in order to uncover their identity, was not taken, as the cost was deemed excessive given that, although the postings were quite bad, they were just not bad enough to go to court over.

Hence, the case was closed, incomplete as it was, much to the chagrin of the investigator, as investigators do not like unfinished cases. Company policy will, alas, always prevail when it comes to private customers.

### *In-depth explanation*

This case shows that perpetrators can hide quite effectively from a private investigation, but would ultimately not be able to escape the law. While it would be easy for a prosecutor to obtain a search warrant allowing analysis of all systems and traffic to the forum site, the private investigator will either have to rely on superior technical means, shady means or social engineering, to get the information. Sometimes, you simply cannot get the job done, which is just a fact of life for an investigator, though everyone hates to admit it. Furthermore, as the company, your customer, always owns the investigation, their will is your command (as the investigator) and when you are ordered to stop, you do just that, however unwilling you may be.

## 9: Case Studies from Large Corporations

Technically, this case illustrates that, except for legal stipulations included in contracts, NDAs or acceptable use policies, there is no way to stop an employee from posting his opinion in some online forum. If that employee had crossed the line to exchange insider information in the legal sense of the word, then criminal proceedings would have been unavoidable, but since the case had caused comparatively little harm, the decision ultimately taken by the company becomes understandable; maybe not acceptable, but understandable.

**The software vulnerability that was not – a case of blackmail**

This case amply illustrates how difficult it has become to resolve today's crime schemes if they are based entirely on IT.

Another company, once again providing online services, would have been perfectly happy just serving its customers, if only the bad guys had left it in peace. Unfortunately, that just didn't happen.

It all started when the company introduced new software for its online services. Some of their software could be used without charge, while some of it needed to be paid for. Now, it turned out that the free software had a bug which a user could take advantage of, and use defraud other users. Since no money was involved, there was, strictly speaking, no damage whatsoever.

One clever person discovered the bug, however, and contacted the company about it. That was fine and the company was grateful for the information. When the issue of financial compensation was raised, the company's first

## 9: Case Studies from Large Corporations

reaction was, 'No problem in receiving compensation, just send us an invoice.' For services such as pointing out a software flaw, no one in the business would expect the invoice to amount to more than 2,000 to 3,000 euros.

The finder, however, did not send an invoice. Instead, his line of argument was that the company had made about x million euros that year and he felt that, for pointing out the bug, he deserved a total of 2.5 million euros. That was a pretty impudent demand, given that the bug only affected free software, and the charged-for software did not have the bug. Things started to get worse from there. As the company did not react to that demand, the person stepped things up a little. He now threatened to expose the company via online forums and YouTube if they did not comply with his demands. By doing this, he crossed the line from impudence to extortion.

So the investigators were called in; only a lead investigator and a second investigator this time, as the case was not deemed big enough to require a full team. The perpetrator was from another European country with a rather weak judicial infrastructure and a different language. The perpetrator was not really able to speak English, which complicated matters quite a bit, as a native language speaker then had to be included in the investigation team. Once that had been done, negotiations were begun, and the perpetrator then posted incriminating videos on YouTube, which meant opening a full criminal case in that country.

So the chief investigator travelled there, established contact with local lawyers and got the proceedings under way. A legal brief was filed with the authorities, outlining and detailing the case, but due to the nature of the country there was no real hope of any fast action on the part of the legal system.

In the meantime, the investigators were successful in getting closer to the perpetrator by using local sources; however, the basic result was that the company he claimed to work for did not exist. It was neither in the UK, where he claimed the headquarters were, nor in his local country. He was using stolen SIM cards to make his calls – it was just not credible that the calls should be coming from a Pakistani illegal immigrant, or from an 80-year-old lady living in the countryside. The identity of the person was still a mystery.

This was to change, quite some time later, as the man established contact with one of the company directors, who had accidentally accepted him as a friend on Facebook. Now a name and a picture were available, although the name did not seem authentic. On the plus side, the lawyers were successful in getting the defamatory videos pulled off YouTube and in having the perpetrator's account suspended. The threat was quite effectively dealt with.

As the company did not react to any of his demands, the perpetrator's will seemed to weaken, but it was revived when the company announced that it was acquiring a similar company in the perpetrator's country. This time, the embarrassing phone calls and blackmailing e-mails were sent to the CEO of the new company as well. The investigation teams managed to contain the threat in a joint action, however, and interest on the perpetrator's part died down again.

As of 2013, the legal case is still continuing and, due to the slowness of the legal system of that country, it is expected to carry on for quite some time. Speedy action on the

## 9: Case Studies from Large Corporations

lawyers' part was, and is, essential to contain the threat and to deal with it appropriately.

It should be mentioned that all proceedings showed clear signs that the perpetrator was an amateur, as a professional extortionist would not just let his interest die down because the victim did not react. Still, even an amateur was able to give the company a severe headache, given that modern IT technology was available to him and that, as it turned out, you can hide your identity quite effectively for some time in that country.

### *In-depth explanation*

Once again, this case amply illustrates the complexities of international investigations and of perpetrators hiding behind borders and weak legislation. It is deplorable that, even among European countries and all those who have signed the Convention on Cybercrime, the ways that organisations are supposed to following up on cybercrime differ so much that they can be deemed ineffective in some countries.

This particular case also shows how superior a well-functioning private investigation team can be when it has all the right contacts in place. The main aspects of this case are outlined below.

The investigation team consisted of a core team of two people and a local contact co-ordinator who synchronised all local sources of information. This group turned out to be strong enough to establish all basic facts of the case.

Not very long into the investigation it became clear that the matter should go to court, and a local legal office was

## 9: Case Studies from Large Corporations

contracted to deal with the local authorities and to file a criminal complaint.

In this case, the company had to contact the authorities in order to be allowed to invoke reasonable self-defence measures, such as initiating an investigation. If they had not notified the authorities, the case could have turned against them in a very ugly way early on or at the latest when it eventually reached the courts. It could even have meant that all evidence secured throughout the investigation would be deemed void.

Furthermore, it turned out to be fundamental to the legal proceedings that, in that particular country, blackmailing and extortion were loosely defined, and the terms covered a lot more than would have been the case in the company's home country. This was important to know and a very positive factor, as it allowed prosecution of the perpetrator in his home country, where the case was legally considered to be a strong one. Under the law in its own country, on the other hand, the company could not have claimed to have suffered a case of extortion, as the threat of force was still too indirect.

The speed with which the investigational team was able to provide facts, such as the origins of telephone numbers used, proved very useful in providing big-picture views of the case.

Having a native-language speaker on board also proved essential in getting a correct picture of the perpetrator's personality and motives. You should always consider native-language staff on international cases, as they might make all the difference. Your native-language speakers will also, of course, be more able to judge local mentality, which will make all the difference when you need to apply social engineering to steer a perpetrator.

It is astonishing to see how efficient you can be in silencing a threat simply by acting as if you are ignoring it. That worked in this case, aided of course by the lawyers who quickly got all the defamatory material pulled off YouTube. That material was evidence in establishing the extortion scheme, and it therefore had to be preserved carefully, which included storing it on write-once-read-only media and calculating hashes.

The main trick employed here was actually to wear out the perpetrator's willingness to proceed which, again, points to the fact that this was not an habitual criminal, but rather an amateur - although he was fairly professional in hiding his identity.

One tip from the field: if you need to store videos posted on YouTube, you can do so by using a site such as www.keepvid.com. This site allows you to store video from a number of other sites as well by entering a link. Quality may suffer, but at least the evidence is preserved.

**Lessons learned**

There is, unfortunately, not much to mention in regard to lessons learned, as the company already has a very elaborate process to ensure software quality and software security. The investigational process was revised to accommodate those aspects that had arisen from the international nature of this case, especially including native-language speakers in order to be able to communicate, which was a major problem in this case.

# PART 3 – A SAMPLE TREATMENT PROCESS

## CHAPTER 10: A SAMPLE TREATMENT PROCESS

In this part, we will present a treatment process for dealing with a breach. This process is intended for larger companies.

It comprises the major steps below.

1. Gather information
2. Determine extent and damage
3. Establish and conduct investigation
4. Determine mitigation (in parallel with Step 3)
5. Implement mitigation
6. Follow up on investigation results
7. Determine degree of resolution achieved

Now let us look at these steps in detail.

### Step 1 Gather information

This is the initial step. We assume that you have just been made aware of the fact that something might be wrong.

You will spend the next hours or days determining precisely what this 'something' is. For example, is it:

- a virus attack?
- a Distributed Denial of Service (DDOS) attack?
- a break-in?
- a lost or stolen piece of hardware (drives, laptops, PCs, servers, paper files)?
- anything else?

## 10: A Sample Treatment Process

So, in the very first step you determine what actually happened. Next, you venture into somewhat legal territory to establish the following points.

- Which sites / jurisdictions are affected?
- Is it:
  - fraud?
  - theft?
  - computer crime?
  - computer or other espionage?
  - anything else?

This is very important, as it will have an influence on later legal proceedings.

Furthermore, you need to establish the points below:

- Where did it happen?
- Where did it originate? This might be entirely different from the sites that are affected.
- Is it an external or internal threat or a case of collusion? If insiders come under suspicion, the investigation will look entirely different and will be more difficult.
- When did it happen? In computer crime it is not unlikely that you become aware of something that happened months previously, which would seriously complicate the investigation.
- Hints about why it happened.

This last point is, of course, the best starting point for actual remedial measures and to prevent the same type of breach from recurring.

# 10: A Sample Treatment Process

**Step 2  Determine extent and damage**

Based on our risk categories, classify the breach in relation to:

- harm done to the company's reputation with the public and its customers
- purely financial damage
- legal damages, such as class-action lawsuits or exposure to criminal penalties (e.g. in cases of bribery)

Be careful to include damages propagating through business processes, and everything else that you reasonably can. Items should include, but not be limited to:

- direct damage to sites or hardware
- damage caused by a need for overtime
- damage through time lost
- damage from contractual penalties
- damage caused by a need for external consulting

When establishing the magnitude of the breach, make sure to include the following departments of your company, so that they are able to prepare:

- PR, for preparing public and customer-oriented statements;
- the Chief Financial Officer for excess budget clearances needed;
- the Chief Executive Officers;
- local managing directors as required;
- senior staff of affected departments, such as IT and Marketing.

## Step 3 Establish and conduct investigation

In the next step, you first need to determine whether the root cause of the breach is sufficiently known, whether you are exposed to some kind of human action, and whether the magnitude of the case justifies an internal or an external investigation. If you deem this to be true, you should assemble an investigational team, as described below. Based on the sensitivity of the case, it is advisable to use external consultants only, as they will be able to act unhindered by internal affairs and will vanish when the investigation concludes.

The investigational team should contain:

- a senior employee of the company, preferably the Chief Security Officer;
- a leader, who should be an experienced senior professional;
- as many technical investigators and operatives as needed; this will depend entirely on the extent of the case, whether it is national or international, and so on;
- a quality assurance officer, who should also be an experienced senior investigation professional.

The leader of the investigation should report to the Chief Security Officer, and the team will typically meet:

- once per day in comparatively easy cases or in cases where external information gathering has anyway to be awaited;
- twice per day if a single day is supposed to bring about significant progress or developments in the case.

Make sure that you have regular progress reports at least weekly.

# 10: A Sample Treatment Process

Looking at the details of an investigation, the subjects can be so different, as the case studies show, that we can say only one thing: each investigation is totally unique. There are groups, based on types of incidents, but there is certainly no such thing as a 'standard' investigation.

You should try to gather all the facts in a central paper and/or electronic file. A well-organised file will contain:

- information on all relevant people (i.e. the targets of the investigation), including full and previous names, addresses, dates of birth and all collected background information;
- information on all relevant places, such as homes, offices and meeting places;
- a list of items of evidence collected and a description of why these are relevant as evidence;
- a description and progress notes of the case;
- a draft criminal complaint or a description of the case suitable for filing a lawsuit against the perpetrator.

**Step 4 Determine mitigation**

This step is conducted in parallel with Step 3, as you would not want to wait for an investigation to conclude before you start thinking about mitigation of the breach.

When determining mitigation you need to think along two lines:

1 What measures will limit the extent of the breach?
2 What measures will prevent the breach, or the entire class of breaches, from happening again?

## 10: A Sample Treatment Process

You will find that immediate measures of containment are usually quite different from those established for a more permanent result. Also, a measure such as a network lockdown will naturally be lifted after some time. Think of 9/11 for example: a nationwide grounding of all air traffic was enforced. While this measure certainly prevents other potential attackers from getting into the air, it makes no sense in the long run, as you cannot prolong it indefinitely.

More permanent measures will include:

- establishing new policies or procedures;
- implementing new technology, such as retinal scanners, better man traps and two-factor authentication;
- relocating a site to a less exposed area of a country or town.

When determining measures, make sure that the root cause(s) are known and well understood, as any measures derived from falsely assumed root causes will not provide any pre-emptive effect.

Be sure also to determine the cost of the measures, and their effectiveness in regard to the breach or class of breaches. Cost effectiveness by itself is not really that important, as the first consideration needs to be whether the measure is effective at all. Remember, though, that while a measure may seem at first sight not to be cost effective, it may still be so in preventing damage that is hard to measure, such as loss of reputation. In the end, it will come down to an executive decision on what protection, against which kind of damage, takes priority and is therefore allowed to incur substantial costs.

# 10: A Sample Treatment Process

**Step 5 Implement mitigation**

Once you have successfully determined what to do, you should implement the measures without undue delay. You would not necessarily implement permanent measures immediately, as this depends on the complexity of the measures and the nature of the changes that they will bring along. If, for example, you choose to alter the organisational structure of your company as a result of a large-scale bribery scheme, you might encounter greater internal resistance than if you were to just set up another internal firewall.

The emphasis, therefore, is on 'without undue delay' as, if the breach is severe enough, your external auditors will certainly question you about the measures taken.

Implementing mitigation measures also includes all those company departments mentioned in Step 2 of this sample process. So, for example, PR could publish a press statement, the CEO might talk to the press, IT could implement its new firewall, the head of internal auditing might be fired for overlooking the root cause that led to the breach, a project on establishing a new policy and associated measures and training might be launched, and so on.

**Step 6 Follow up on investigation results**

It is quite obvious that not all investigations can be completed successfully. This means that you need to regularly follow up on the investigation's results, and to study any kind of final result carefully and act accordingly.

## 10: A Sample Treatment Process

Following up also includes going to court or, in more general terms, putting the results of the investigation to best use for the company in the strategic and tactical context.

You should be aware that the legal steps following a breach are usually extremely time consuming. It is not unusual for legal proceedings to go on for as long as two years before a final verdict is reached, and it can take even longer in large corporate cases.

### Step 7 Determine degree of resolution achieved

Once you have resolved the breach and implemented the measures that you have identified, it is of paramount importance to determine whether these measures have been effective. This is part of ISO27001's requirement to learn from incidents and, generally, is just plain good practice. Any measure you have implemented cannot be deemed effective just because you have not suffered another breach for a while; that is definitely not enough. You need to look actively at how the measures have been implemented and to audit them in full.

You may even wish to bring in external auditors, so that you can gain an unbiased view. In general, the more complex the measures you have implemented, the more beneficial it will be to have an external review in addition to your internal one.

If you find that the measures have not been implemented as designed, then you must act again without undue delay.

# ABBREVIATIONS AND ACRONYMS

| | |
|---|---|
| AL | Acceptable Loss |
| ALE | Annual Loss Expectancy |
| CMDB | Configuration Management Database |
| BCP | Business Continuity Plan |
| CFO | Chief Finance Officer |
| CISO | Chief Information Security Officer |
| COO | Chief Operating Officer |
| CSO | Chief Security Officer |
| DNS | Domain Name System |
| FSA | Financial Services Authority |
| IS | Information Security |
| ISP | Internet Service Provider |
| ITIL® | Information Technology Infrastructure Library |
| NDA | Non-Disclosure Agreement |
| NSA | National Security Agency |
| NTFS | New Technology File System |
| OS | Operating System |
| PGP | Pretty Good Privacy |
| WAN | Wide Area Network |
| WLAN | Wireless Local Area Network |

# ITG RESOURCES

IT Governance Ltd sources, creates and delivers products and services to meet the real-world, evolving IT governance needs of today's organisations, directors, managers and practitioners.

The ITG website (*www.itgovernance.co.uk*) is the international one-stop-shop for corporate and IT governance information, advice, guidance, books, tools, training and consultancy. On the website you will find the following pages related to the subject matter of this book:

*www.itgovernance.co.uk/infosec.aspx*

*www.itgovernance.co.uk/iso27001.aspx*.

**Publishing Services**

IT Governance Publishing (ITGP) is the world's leading IT-GRC publishing imprint that is wholly owned by IT Governance Ltd.

With books and tools covering all IT governance, risk and compliance frameworks, we are the publisher of choice for authors and distributors alike, producing unique and practical publications of the highest quality, in the latest formats available, which readers will find invaluable.

*www.itgovernancepublishing.co.uk* is the website dedicated to ITGP. Other titles published by ITGP that may be of interest include:

- Once more unto the Breach

    *www.itgovernance.co.uk/shop/p-985.aspx*

- Information Security Breaches: Avoidance and Treatment based on ISO27001

    *www.itgovernance.co.uk/shop/p-601.aspx*

## ITG Resources

- The True Cost of Information Security Breaches and Cyber Crime

  *www.itgovernance.co.uk/shop/p-1338.aspx*.

We also offer a range of off-the-shelf toolkits that give comprehensive, customisable documents to help users create the specific documentation they need to properly implement a management system or standard. Written by experienced practitioners and based on the latest best practice, ITGP toolkits can save months of work for organisations working towards compliance with a given standard.

To see the full range of toolkits available please visit:

*www.itgovernance.co.uk/shop/c-129-toolkits.aspx*.

Books and tools published by IT Governance Publishing (ITGP) are available from all business booksellers and the following websites:

*www.itgovernance.eu*   *www.itgovernanceusa.com*
*www.itgovernance.in*   *www.itgovernancesa.co.za*
*www.itgovernance.asia*.

**Training Services**

IT Governance offers an extensive portfolio of training courses designed to educate information security, IT governance, risk management and compliance professionals. Our classroom and online training programmes will help you develop the skills required to deliver best practice and compliance to your organisation. They will also enhance your career by providing you with industry standard certifications and increased peer recognition. Our range of courses offer a structured learning path from Foundation to Advanced level in the key topics of

## ITG Resources

information security, IT governance, business continuity and service management.

ISO/IEC 27001:2013 is the international management standard that helps businesses and organisations throughout the world develop a best-in-class Information Security Management System. Knowledge and experience in implementing and maintaining ISO27001 compliance are considered to be essential to building a successful career in information security. We have the world's first programme of certificated ISO27001 education with Foundation, Lead Implementer, Risk Management and Lead Auditor training courses. Each course is designed to provide delegates with relevant knowledge and skills and an industry-recognised qualification awarded by the International Board for IT Governance Qualifications (IBITGQ).

Full details of all IT Governance training courses can be found at www.itgovernance.co.uk/training.aspx.

**Professional Services and Consultancy**

Your mission to plug critical security gaps will be greatly assisted by IT Governance consultants, who have advised hundreds of information security managers in the adoption of ISO27001 Information Security Management Systems (ISMS).

The organisation's assets, security and data systems, not to mention its reputation, are all in your hands. A major security breach could spell disaster. Timely advice and support from IT governance experts will enable you to identify the threats, assess risks and put in place the necessary controls before there's an incident.

At IT Governance, we understand that information, information security and information technology are always business issues, and not just IT ones. Our consultancy services assist you in managing information security strategies in

## ITG Resources

harmony with business goals, conveying the right messages to your colleagues to support decision-making.

For more information about IT Governance Consultancy, see: *www.itgovernance.co.uk/consulting.aspx*.

**Newsletter**

IT governance is one of the hottest topics in business today, not least because it is also the fastest moving.

You can stay up to date with the latest developments across the whole spectrum of IT governance subject matter, including; risk management, information security, ITIL and IT service management, project governance, compliance and so much more, by subscribing to ITG's core publications and topic alert emails.

Simply visit our subscription centre and select your preferences: *www.itgovernance.co.uk/newsletter.aspx*.

EU for product safety is Stephen Evans, The Mill Enterprise Hub, Stagreenan, Drogheda, Co. Louth, A92 CD3D, Ireland. (servicecentre@itgovernance.eu)

www.ingramcontent.com/pod-product-compliance
Lightning Source LLC
Chambersburg PA
CBHW061446300426
44114CB00014B/1852